I0408236

Pocket Guide Overview

POCKET GUIDE OVERVIEW

Intended patient outcomes of the VA/DoD Clinical Practice Guideline for the Management of Post-traumatic Stress (PTS) and Posttraumatic Stress Disorder (PTSD) Pocket Guide:

- Improvement in symptoms, quality of life, and social and occupational functioning for those with PTS and PTSD
- Improvement of patient engagement and satisfaction
- Improvement in co-occurring conditions
- Reduction in morbidity/mortality

Department of Veterans Affairs (VA) and Department of Defense (DoD) employees who use this information are responsible for considering all applicable regulations and policies throughout the course of care and patient education.

Background

- For more comprehensive information, please refer to the full-length VA/DoD CPG for PTS and 2010 updated summary, available at:
  - healthquality.va.gov/Post_Traumatic_Stress_Disorder_PTSD.asp
  - https://www.qmo.amedd.army.mil/ptsd/ptsd.html

NOTE: The pocket guide recommendations are intended to support clinical decision-making but should never replace sound clinical judgment.

VA/DoD CPG and PTSD Pocket Guide Goals

- Promote improved identification of patients along the spectrum of PTS conditions – including acute stress reaction (ASR), acute stress disorder (ASD), combat and operational stress reaction (COSR), acute PTSD and chronic PTSD
- Promote early treatment, engagement and retention of patients with PTSD and related conditions who can benefit from treatment

Target Audience and Patient Population

- Health care professionals who provide or direct treatment services to adult patients with PTSD and related conditions in any VA or DoD healthcare setting

Tabs in the Pocket Guide

The Pocket Guide references steps from the CPG that address interrelated aspects of care for patients with PTSD and related conditions:

Tab 2	**Initial Evaluation and Triage** Includes information on the PTS spectrum, trauma, prevention of PTSD, and education and normalization about symptoms
Tab 3	**Acute Stress Reaction: 0-4 Days** Includes information on assessment for ASR, ensuring basic physical needs are met and psychological first aid (PFA)
Tab 4	**Combat and Operational Stress Reaction: 0-4 Days** Includes information on assessment and follow-up for COSR
Tab 5	**Acute Stress Disorder: >2-30 Days** Includes information on assessment for ASD, acute interventions, reassessment and follow-up
Tab 6	**Assessment and Diagnosis of Posttraumatic Stress Disorder: >1 month** Includes information on assessment, diagnosis, education, and determining care and treatment
Tab 7	**Management of Posttraumatic Stress Disorder: >1 month** Includes information on evidence-based treatment, adjunctive therapies, reassessment and follow-up

| Tab 8 | **Medication Tables**
Includes information on evidence-based pharmacotherapy treatment |
| Tab 9 | **Additional Tools & Resources** |

The table below details strength of evidence-base as outlined in the VA/DoD CPG for PTS. Recommendations throughout this pocket guide will reference the strength of recommendation as defined in this table.

STRENGTH OF RECOMMENDATION	
A	**A strong recommendation that clinicians provide the intervention to eligible patients.** Good evidence was found that the intervention improves important health outcomes and concludes that benefits substantially outweigh harm.
B	**A recommendation that clinicians provide (the service) to eligible patients.** At least fair evidence was found that the intervention improves health outcomes and concludes that benefits outweigh harm.
C	**No recommendation for or against the routine provision of the intervention is made.** At least fair evidence was found that the intervention can improve health outcomes, but concludes that the balance of benefits and harm is too close to justify a general recommendation.
D	**A recommendation is made against routinely providing the intervention to asymptomatic patients.** At least fair evidence was found that the intervention is ineffective or that harm outweighs benefits.
I	**The conclusion is that the evidence is insufficient to recommend for or against routinely providing the intervention.** Evidence that the intervention is effective is lacking, of poor quality, or conflicting, and the balance of benefits and harm cannot be determined.

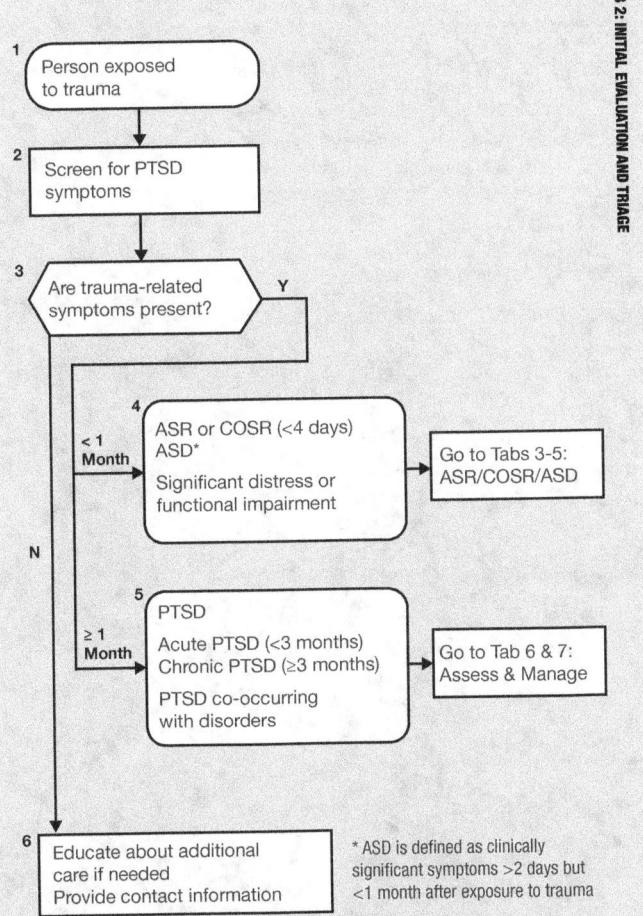

1 Person exposed to trauma

2 Screen for PTSD symptoms

3 Are trauma-related symptoms present? — Y

< 1 Month

4 ASR or COSR (<4 days)
ASD*

Significant distress or functional impairment

→ Go to Tabs 3-5: ASR/COSR/ASD

≥ 1 Month

5 PTSD

Acute PTSD (<3 months)
Chronic PTSD (≥3 months)

PTSD co-occurring with disorders

→ Go to Tab 6 & 7: Assess & Manage

N

6 Educate about additional care if needed
Provide contact information

* ASD is defined as clinically significant symptoms >2 days but <1 month after exposure to trauma

Initial Evaluation and Triage

Tab 2:
INITIAL EVALUATION & TRIAGE

PTS is the term used to define the spectrum of conditions that includes COSR, ASR, ASD, and acute and chronic PTSD.

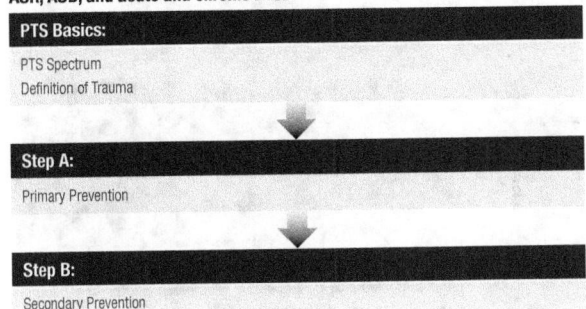

PTS Basics:

PTS Spectrum
Definition of Trauma

Step A:

Primary Prevention

Step B:

Secondary Prevention

Post-traumatic Stress Spectrum Basics

- Each condition in the PTS spectrum is classified according to symptom duration or stressor (e.g., combat)

PTS Spectrum by Symptom Duration

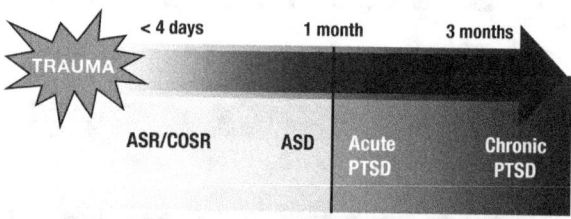

Trauma is defined in the CPG as:

- Direct personal experience of an event that involves actual or threatened death or serious injury or another threat to one's physical integrity
- Witnessing an event that involves death, injury or a threat to the physical integrity of another person
- Learning about unexpected or violent death, serious harm, or threat of death or injury experienced by a family member or other close associate

According to criteria in the Diagnostic and Statistical Manual of Mental Disorders, Fourth Edition (Text Revision) (DSM-IV-TR), the person's response to the event must involve intense fear, helplessness or horror. However, there is evidence that military personnel do not always respond in the same way as civilian victims of traumatic events, and the criteria for "fear, helplessness or horror" are being reconsidered in the proposed future DSM criteria.

(Adler AB, Wright KM, Bliese PD, Eckford R, Hoge CW. A2 diagnostic criterion for combat-related posttraumatic stress disorder. J Trauma Stress. 2008 Jun;21(3):301-8.)

Step A: Primary Prevention

Primary prevention in PTSD involves efforts to reduce risk and enhance protective factors before the individual experiences trauma, or after a trauma and before symptom onset, in order to prevent the development of the disorder.

In high-risk occupations, for which the probability of trauma exposure is moderate or high (e.g., service members, law enforcement personnel, firefighters and medical or emergency first responders), efforts should be undertaken to increase the psychological resilience of workers to the negative effects of trauma.

Foster Resilience in High-Risk Individuals

Resilience can be strengthened through:
- **Realistic, duty-related stress training** (e.g., live-fire exercises, survival and captivity training)
- **Coping skills training** (e.g., relaxation, cognitive reframing and problem-solving skills training)
- **Supportive work environment** (e.g., open team communication and peer support)
- **Adaptive beliefs about the work role and traumatic experiences** (e.g., confidence in leadership and realistic expectancies about work environment)
- **Workplace-specific traumatic stress management programs** (e.g., chaplains and mental health professionals)

Populations at Risk for Developing PTSD

Persons exposed to trauma should be assessed for the type, frequency, nature and severity of the trauma
- Assessment should include a broad range of potential trauma exposures in addition to the index trauma
- Trauma exposure assessment instruments may assist in evaluating the nature and severity of the exposure
- Assessment of existing social supports and ongoing stressors is important

Step B: Secondary Prevention

Secondary prevention involves the earliest possible identification of symptoms, education and early symptom management so that adverse sequelae are reduced or prevented.

All new patients should be screened for symptoms of PTSD initially, and then on an annual basis or more frequently if clinically indicated due to clinical suspicion, recent trauma exposure (e.g., major disaster) or history of PTSD using a validated tool*. For example:
- Primary Care PTSD Screen (PC-PTSD)
- PTSD Brief Screen
- Short Screening Scale for DSM-IV PTSD
- PTSD Checklist (PCL)

*Each measure is validated for use in PTSD screening. There is insufficient evidence to recommend one tool versus another or recommend special screening for minority members.

Survivors or responders who show distressing symptoms or disturbed behavior should be educated to understand that their reactions are common, normal responses to the extreme events. Such an approach follows from the common clinical observation that individuals experiencing acute stress reactions often interpret their reactions as signs of "personal weakness" or evidence that they are "going crazy." Such beliefs may increase their demoralization and distress. Normalization is undermined if survivors or responders who are not experiencing disruptive distress show a derogatory or punitive attitude to others who are.

Recommendations
- Pre- and post-trauma education should include helping the asymptomatic trauma survivor or responder understand that the acute stress reactions of other people are common and probably transient, and do not indicate personal failure or weakness, mental illness or health problems

- Education should include sufficient review of the many ways that post-traumatic problems can present, including symptoms in the ASD/PTSD spectrum, behavioral problems with family and friends, occupational problems, and the potential impact of alcohol or other substance misuse/abuse
- Education should also include positive messages by identifying and encouraging positive ways of coping, describing simple strategies to resolve or cope with developing symptoms and problems, and setting expectations for mastery and/or recovery
- Provide contact information, should post-traumatic symptoms emerge later
- Routine debriefing or formal psychotherapy is not beneficial for asymptomatic individuals and may be harmful

Common Signs & Symptoms Following Exposure to Trauma

Physical	Cognitive/Mental	Emotional	Behavioral
■ Chills	■ Blaming someone	■ Agitation	■ Increased alcohol consumption
■ Difficulty breathing	■ Change in alertness	■ Anxiety	■ Antisocial acts
■ Dizziness	■ Confusion	■ Apprehension	■ Change in activity
■ Elevated blood pressure	■ Hypervigilance	■ Denial	■ Change in communication
■ Fainting	■ Increased or decreased awareness of surroundings	■ Depression	■ Change in sexual functioning
■ Fatigue	■ Intrusive images	■ Emotional shock	■ Change in speech pattern
■ Grinding teeth	■ Memory problems	■ Fear	■ Emotional outbursts
■ Headaches	■ Nightmares	■ Feeling overwhelmed	■ Inability to rest
■ Muscle tremors	■ Poor abstract thinking	■ Grief	■ Change in appetite
■ Nausea	■ Poor attention	■ Guilt	■ Pacing
■ Pain	■ Poor concentration	■ Inappropriate emotional response	■ Intensified startle reflex
■ Profuse sweating	■ Poor decision-making	■ Irritability	■ Suspiciousness
■ Rapid heart rate	■ Poor problem solving	■ Loss of emotional control	■ Social withdrawal
■ Twitches			
■ Weakness			

Page intentionally left blank

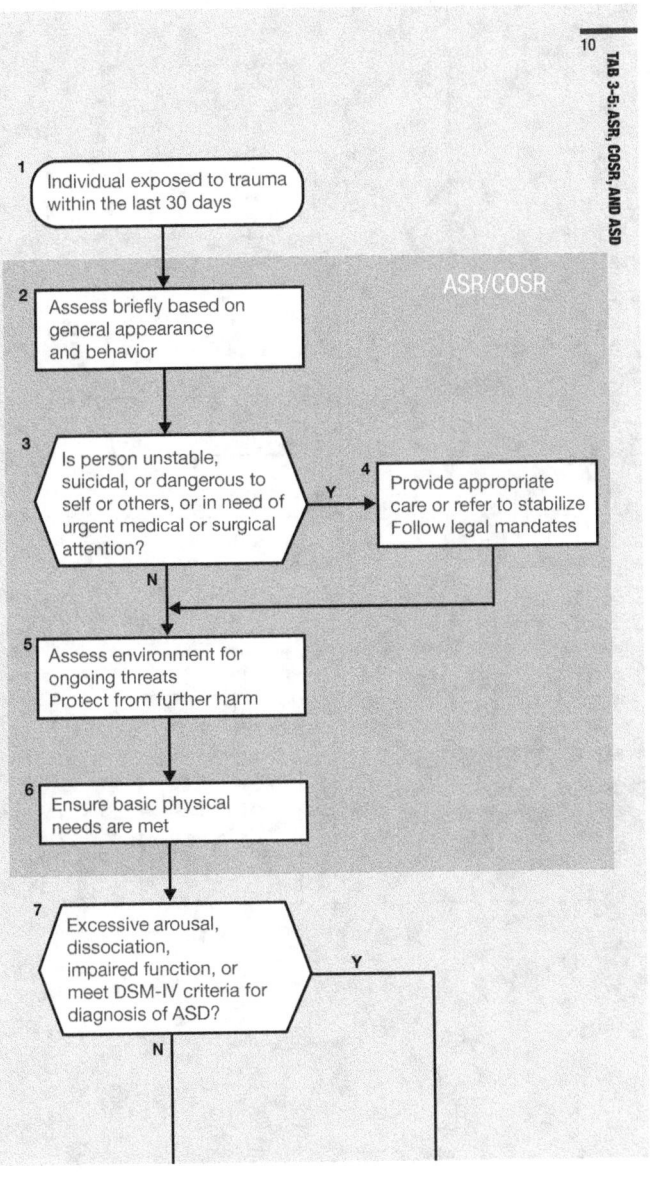

1 Individual exposed to trauma within the last 30 days

2 Assess briefly based on general appearance and behavior

ASR/COSR

3 Is person unstable, suicidal, or dangerous to self or others, or in need of urgent medical or surgical attention?

Y → 4 Provide appropriate care or refer to stabilize Follow legal mandates

N

5 Assess environment for ongoing threats Protect from further harm

6 Ensure basic physical needs are met

7 Excessive arousal, dissociation, impaired function, or meet DSM-IV criteria for diagnosis of ASD?

Y

N

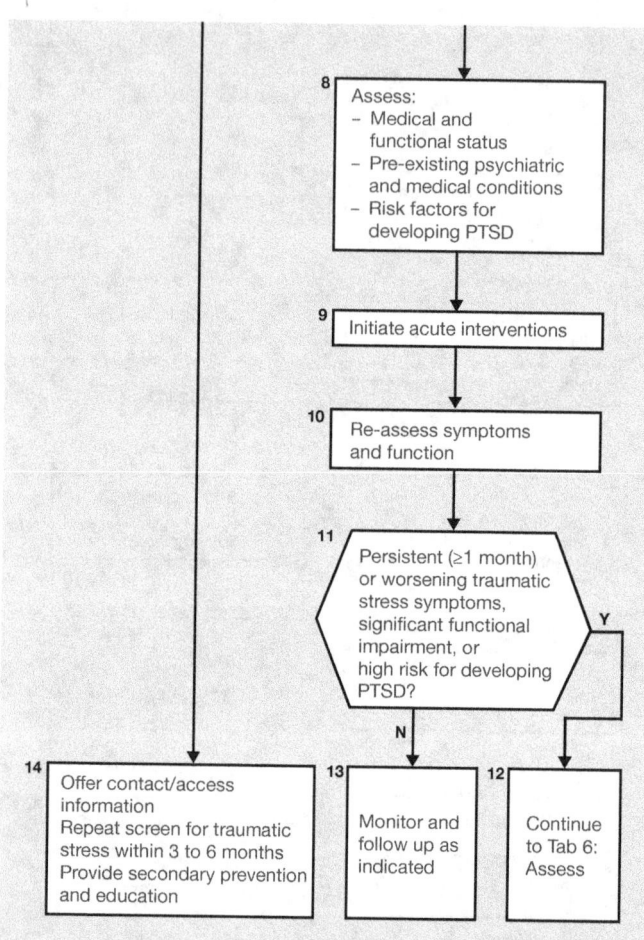

8 Assess:
- Medical and functional status
- Pre-existing psychiatric and medical conditions
- Risk factors for developing PTSD

9 Initiate acute interventions

10 Re-assess symptoms and function

11 Persistent (≥1 month) or worsening traumatic stress symptoms, significant functional impairment, or high risk for developing PTSD?

Y

N

14 Offer contact/access information
Repeat screen for traumatic stress within 3 to 6 months
Provide secondary prevention and education

13 Monitor and follow up as indicated

12 Continue to Tab 6: Assess

Page intentionally left blank

Acute Stress Reaction: 0 – 4 Days

Tab 3:
ACUTE STRESS REACTION: 0-4 DAYS

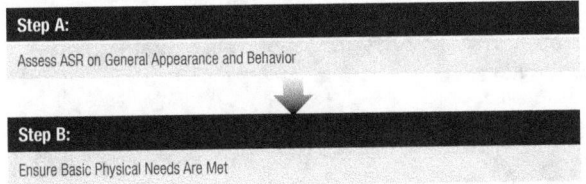

Step A:

Assess ASR on General Appearance and Behavior

Step B:

Ensure Basic Physical Needs Are Met

Acute stress reaction is a transient condition that often develops within zero to four days from exposure to a traumatic event. Onset of at least some signs and symptoms may be simultaneous with the trauma itself, within minutes of the traumatic event, or may follow the trauma after an interval of hours or days. In most cases, symptoms will disappear within days.

Step A: Assess ASR on General Appearance and Behavior

- Individuals involved in a traumatic event exhibiting the following responses should be screened for ASR (no specific screening tool is recommended):
  - **Physical:** exhaustion, hyperarousal, somatic complaints or symptoms of conversion disorder
  - **Emotional:** anxiety, depression, guilt/hopelessness
  - **Cognitive:** amnestic or dissociative symptoms, hypervigilance, paranoia, intrusive re-experiencing
  - **Behavioral:** avoidance, problematic substance use

- Conduct a comprehensive assessment of symptoms that includes:
  - Details about the time of onset
  - Frequency and course
  - Severity and level of distress
  - Functional impairment
  - Capability to perform routine functions

Protect

- Address acute medical and behavioral issues to preserve life and avoid further harm
  - Provide appropriate medical/surgical care
  - Assess danger to self or others (e.g., suicidal or homicidal behavior)
- Arrange a safe, private and comfortable environment for the continuation of the evaluation
- Follow legal mandates (see below for examples)
- Consider interventions to secure safety
- Educate and "normalize" observed psychological reactions to the chain of command
- Elevate to the next level of care if:
  - Symptoms are unmanageable
  - Existing resources are unavailable
  - Reaction is outside the scope of expertise of the care provider

Legal mandates should be followed:	Reporting of violence or assault
	Confidentiality of the patient
	Attending to chain of evidence in criminal cases (e.g., rape, evaluation)
	Involuntary commitment procedures, if needed
	Mandatory testing

Step B: Ensure Basic Physical Needs Are Met

Acute intervention should ensure that the following needs are met:

- Safety, security and survival
- Food, hydration, clothing, hygiene and shelter
- Sleep
- Medications (i.e., replace medications destroyed or lost)
- Education as to current status
- Communication with family, friends and community
- Protection from ongoing threats, toxins and harm. If indicated, reduce use of alcohol, tobacco, caffeine and illicit psychoactive substances

EARLY INTERVENTIONS AFTER EXPOSURE TO TRAUMA
(0 – 4 DAYS AFTER EXPOSURE)

Effect = Balance of Benefit and Harm				
SR	Significant Benefit	Some Benefit	Unknown Benefit	No Benefit Potential Harm
I	–	• Psychological first aid (PFA) • Psychoeducation and normalization • Social support	• Spiritual support	–
D	–	–	–	• Psychological debriefing

SR = Strength of recommendation
I = Insufficient evidence
D = Ineffective or harmful

Psychological first aid (PFA) is an identified early intervention after exposure to trauma. Provide PFA to:

- Protect survivors from future harm
- Reduce physiological arousal
- Mobilize support for those who are most distressed
- Keep families together and facilitate reunion with loved ones
- Provide information and foster communication and education
- Use effective risk communication techniques

KEY ELEMENTS OF PFA

- **Contact and engagement** - Respond to contact initiated by affected persons, or initiate contact in a non-intrusive, compassionate and helpful manner
- **Safety and comfort** - Enhance immediate and ongoing safety, and provide physical and emotional comfort
- **Stabilization (if needed)** - Calm and orient emotionally overwhelmed or distraught survivors
- **Information gathering** - Identify immediate needs and concerns, gather additional information and tailor PFA interventions
- **Practical assistance** - Offer practical help to the survivor in addressing immediate needs and concerns
- **Connection with social supports** - Help establish opportunities for brief or ongoing contacts with primary support persons or other sources of support, including family members, friends and community help resources
- **Information on coping** - Provide information (about stress reactions and coping) to reduce distress and promote adaptive functioning
- **Linkage to collaborative services** - Link survivors with needed services and inform them about available services that may be needed in the future

These core goals of PFA constitute the basic objectives of providing early assistance (e.g., within days or weeks following an event). The amount of time spent on each goal will vary from person to person and with different circumstances, according to need.

The complete document describing PFA components can be found at: vdh.virginia.gov

Page intentionally left blank

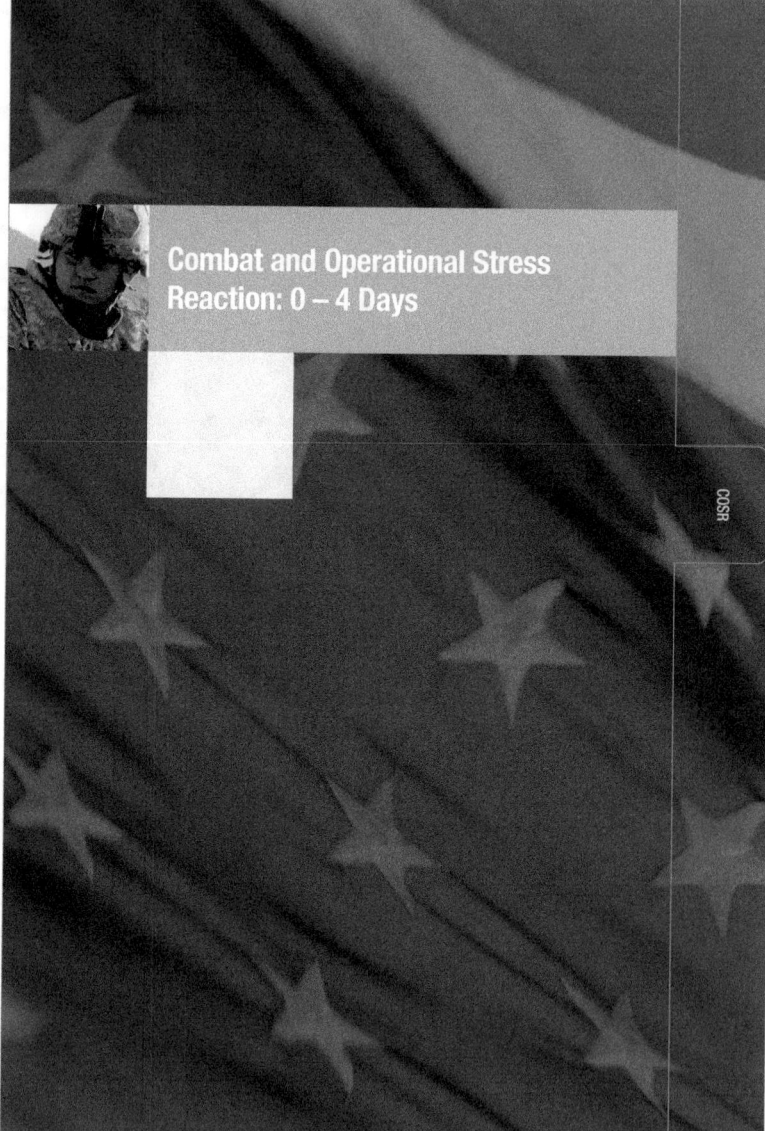

Combat and Operational Stress Reaction: 0 – 4 Days

Tab 4:

COMBAT AND OPERATIONAL STRESS REACTION (COSR): 0 – 4 DAYS

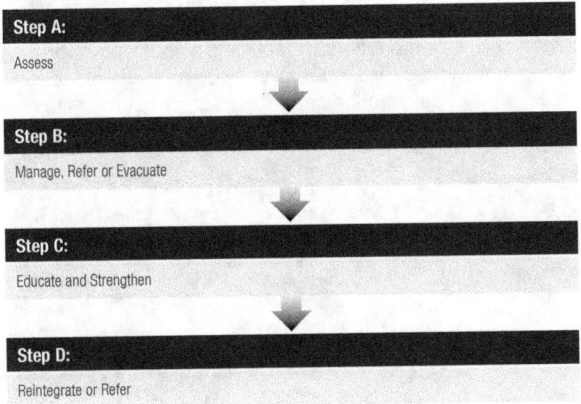

Step A:

Assess

Step B:

Manage, Refer or Evacuate

Step C:

Educate and Strengthen

Step D:

Reintegrate or Refer

Step A: Assess

COSR is the term used to describe an ASR in the combat environment and can include virtually any symptom and sign, including physical and neurological symptoms, resulting from exposure to extremely stressful events or combat experiences. It may result from specific traumatic experiences in combat or exhaustion due to the cumulative effects of one or more factors, including sleep deprivation, extreme physical stress, poor sanitary conditions, limited caloric intake, dehydration or extremes of environmental conditions. It is a common response and not an illness.

Identify

- Individuals involved in traumatic events, including:
  - Combat in a war zone, ongoing military operations, and continuous or recurring exposure to traumatic events
- Individuals who were involved in events specific to COSR:
  - Intense emotional demands (e.g., rescue personnel and caregivers searching for possibly dying survivors or interacting with bereaved family members)
  - Extreme fatigue, weather exposure, hunger or sleep deprivation
  - Extended exposure to danger, loss, and emotional or physical strain
  - Exposure to environmental hazards, such as toxic contamination
  - Cumulative exposure to multiple stressors

Assess

- Service member's role and functional capabilities and the complexity and importance of his or her job
- Functional status to include:
  - Any significant changes in work performance
  - Co-worker or supervisor reports of recent changes in appearance, quality of work or relationships
  - Signs of loss of motivation, loss of interest or unreliability
  - Signs of forgetfulness and distraction
  - Substance use

Step A: Assess (cont.)

- Service member's role and functional capabilities and the complexity and importance of his or her job
- Symptoms of COSR
- Collateral information from unit leaders, co-workers or peers about:
  - Stressors
  - Function
  - Medical history
  - Absence or impairment in operation or mission

Step B: Manage, Refer or Evacuate

Combat Operation Stress Control (COSC) utilizes the management principles of brevity, immediacy, contact, expectancy, proximity and simplicity (BICEPS). These principles apply to all COSC interventions or activities throughout the theater and are followed by personnel in all psychological health COSC elements. These principles may be applied differently based on a particular level of care and other factors pertaining to mission, enemy, terrain and weather, troops and support available, time available, and civil considerations.

Another mnemonic that is often used in the management of COSR is the six Rs.

The Six Rs	
Reassure	normality (normalize the reaction)
Rest	from combat or break from work
Replenish	bodily needs (such as thermal comfort, water, food, hygiene and sleep)
Restore	confidence with purposeful activities and talk

Retain	contact with fellow service members and unit
Remind/ Recognize	the emotion of the reaction (specifically potentially life-threatening thoughts and behaviors)

For additional information see COSR protocols for DoD-specific services.

Step C: Educate and Strengthen

Help individuals cope with COSR by providing information that may help them manage their symptoms and benefit from treatment.

All individuals should be given educational information to help normalize common reactions to trauma, improve coping, enhance self-care, facilitate recognition of significant problems, and increase knowledge of and access to services.

Step D: Reintegrate or Refer

Each of the armed services offers special support services in the field. These teams evaluate, treat and educate service members affected by combat stress; in most cases, these teams help service members return to their units without referring them to higher levels of care. Service members with COSR who do not respond to initial supportive interventions may warrant referral or evacuation.

Page intentionally left blank

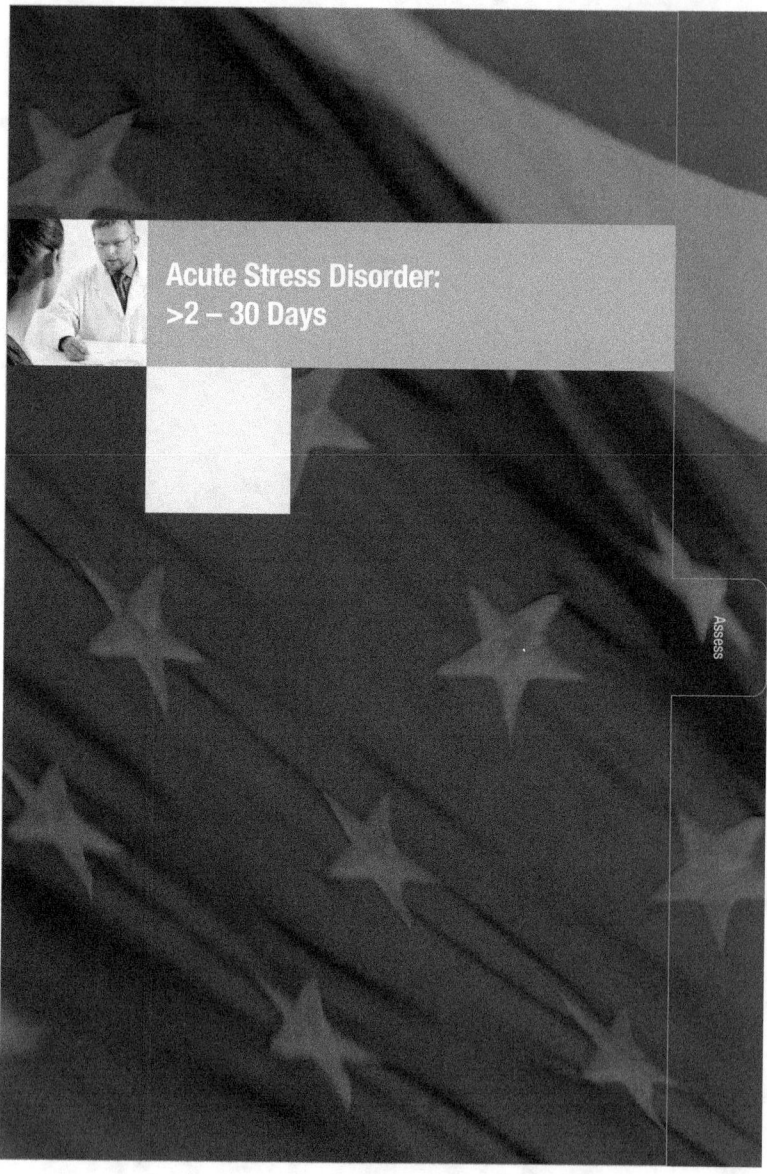

Acute Stress Disorder:
>2 – 30 Days

ACUTE STRESS DISORDER: >2 – 30 DAYS

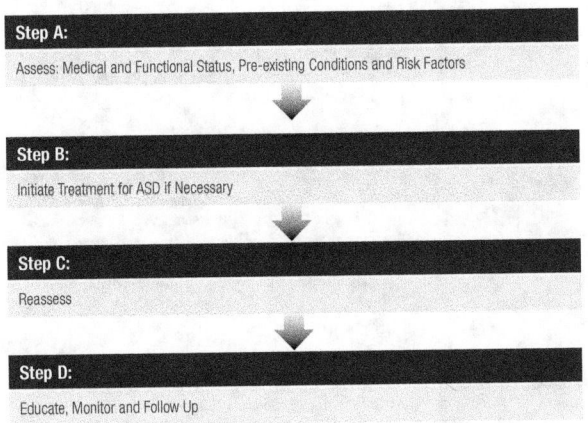

Step A:

Assess: Medical and Functional Status, Pre-existing Conditions and Risk Factors

Step B:

Initiate Treatment for ASD if Necessary

Step C:

Reassess

Step D:

Educate, Monitor and Follow Up

Step A: Assess: Medical and Functional Status, Pre-existing Conditions and Risk Factors

Identify

- Acutely traumatized people who meet the criteria for diagnosis of ASD (see Tab 9: Resources, for diagnostic criteria; there is insufficient evidence to recommend one screening tool versus another)
- Those with sub-threshold but significant symptoms two weeks post-trauma
- Those who are incapacitated by acute psychological or physical symptoms

Assess Medical and Functional Status

- Medical: history, physical exam, neurological exam
- Based on clinical presentation, may include toxicology screen, radiological assessment, lab studies to rule out medical disorders that may cause symptoms of ASD (e.g., chemistry profile, thyroid studies)
- Psychosocial: active stressors, losses, current social supports and basic needs
- Functional: general appearance and behavior, subjectively impaired function, baseline level of function (LOF) vs. current LOF, family and relationship functioning

Assess Pre-Existing Conditions

- Assess patients by clinical interview for pre-existing psychological conditions (e.g., past history of PTSD, major depressive disorder, substance use disorder (SUD)) to identify high-risk individuals and groups
  - See the VA/DoD CPGs for major depressive disorder and SUD for more information on assessment (healthquality.va.gov/index.asp & https://www.qmo.amedd.army.mil/pguide.htm)
- Assure access and adherence to medications that the patient is currently taking
- Refer patients with pre-existing psychological conditions to psychological health specialty when indicated or emergency hospitalization, if needed

Assess Risk Factors

- Trauma survivors who exhibit symptoms or functional impairment should be screened for the following risk factors for developing ASD and PTSD:
  - Pre-traumatic factors
  - Peri-traumatic or trauma-related factors
  - Post-traumatic factors

For risk factor examples, see chart on the following page.

EXAMPLES OF RISK FACTORS FOR DEVELOPING ASD AND PTSD:

Pre-traumatic Factors

- Ongoing life stress
- Lack of social support
- Young age at time of trauma
- Pre-existing psychological conditions or substance misuse *or* family history of psychological conditions
- History of traumatic events or abuse
- History of PTSD

Peri-traumatic or Trauma-related Factors

- Severe trauma
- Physical injury to self or others
- High-risk trauma (e.g., combat, killing another person, torture, rape, assault)
- High perceived threat to life of self or others
- Mass trauma
- History of peri-traumatic dissociation

Post-traumatic Factors

- Ongoing life stress
- Lack of positive social support
- Bereavement or traumatic grief
- Major loss of resources
- Negative social support (blaming environment)
- Poor coping skills
- Distressed spouse or children

Step B: Initiate Treatment for ASD if Necessary

Provide Education and Normalization

- ALL individuals should be given information on:
  - Normalizing reactions to trauma
  - Improving coping
  - Enhancing self-care
  - Facilitating recognition of significant problems
  - Increasing knowledge of and access to care

Initiate Brief Intervention

- Brief psychotherapy
- Pharmacotherapy
- See evidence-table on the following page for early interventions after exposure to trauma (four to 30 days after exposure)

Acute Symptom Management

- Consider a short course (less than six days) of medication to treat:
  - Sleep disturbance or insomnia
  - Management of pain
  - Irritation, excessive arousal or anger
- Provide non-pharmacological intervention to address specific symptoms (e.g., relaxation, breathing techniques, avoiding caffeine) to address both general recovery and specific symptoms (e.g., sleep disturbances, pain, hyperarousal, anger)

Facilitate Spiritual and Social Support

- Facilitate patient access to spiritual and social care when sought
- Assess for spiritual needs and impact of ASD on social functioning
- Provide opportunities for grieving as determined by the patient (i.e., providing opportunity for prayer, mantras, rites, rituals, end-of-life care)
- Preserve an interpersonal safety zone (e.g., privacy, quiet)
- Reconnect trauma survivors with supportive relationships

EARLY INTERVENTIONS AFTER EXPOSURE TO TRAUMA
(4 TO 30 DAYS AFTER EXPOSURE)

Effect = Balance of Benefit and Harm				
SR	**Significant Benefit**	**Some Benefit**	**Unknown Benefit**	**No Benefit**
A	■ Brief (four to five sessions) cognitive behavioral therapy (CBT)	–	–	–
B	–	–	–	–
C	–	■ Social support	–	–
D	–	–	–	■ Individual psychological debriefing* ■ Formal psychotherapy for asymptomatic survivors* ■ Benzodiazepines* ■ Typical antipsychotics*
I	–	■ Psychoeducation and normalization	■ Imipramine ■ Propranolol ■ Prazosin ■ Other antidepressants ■ Anticonvulsants ■ Atypical antipsychotics ■ Spiritual support ■ PFA	■ Group psychological debriefing

SR = Strength of recommendation, *potential harm

A = Strong recommendation

B = Fair evidence

C = Fair evidence but no general recommendation

D = Ineffective or harmful

I = Insufficient evidence

> ## Step C: Reassess

REASSESS SYMPTOMS AND FUNCTION

Reassessment should include evaluation of:	▪ Persistent or worsening traumatic symptoms (e.g., panic, dissociation) ▪ Significant functional impairments (e.g., work, relationships) ▪ Dangerousness (i.e., suicidal, violent) ▪ Severe psychiatric co-occurring disorders (e.g., SUD) ▪ Maladaptive coping strategies (e.g., impulsivity, social withdrawal) ▪ New or evolving psychosocial stressors ▪ Poor social supports
Patient does not improve or status worsens:	▪ Continue management of PTSD *or* ▪ Refer to PTSD specialty care or psychological health provider ▪ Involve primary care provider in treatment
Patient demonstrates partial improvement:	▪ Consider augmentation or adjustment of the acute intervention ▪ Follow up within two weeks
Patient recovers from acute symptoms:	▪ Provide education ▪ Provide contact information with instructions for available follow-up, if needed

Step D: Educate, Monitor and Follow Up

Individuals who fail to respond to early interventions should be referred for PTSD treatment when they have:

- Worsening of stress-related symptoms
- High potential for new-onset symptoms or dangerousness
- Maladaptive coping with stress (e.g., social withdrawal)
- Exacerbation of pre-existing psychological conditions
- Deterioration in function
- New-onset stressors
- Poor social supports

The primary care provider should:

- Consider initiating therapy pending referral, or if the patient is reluctant to obtain specialty services
- Continue evaluating and treating co-occurring physical illnesses, and addressing any other health concerns
- Educate and validate the patient regarding his or her illness

Follow-up should be offered to those who request it or to individuals who:

- Have ASD or other clinically significant symptoms stemming from the trauma
- Are bereaved
- Have a pre-existing psychological disorder
- Require medical or surgical attention
- Were exposed to a major incident or disaster that was particularly intense and of long duration

Page intentionally left blank

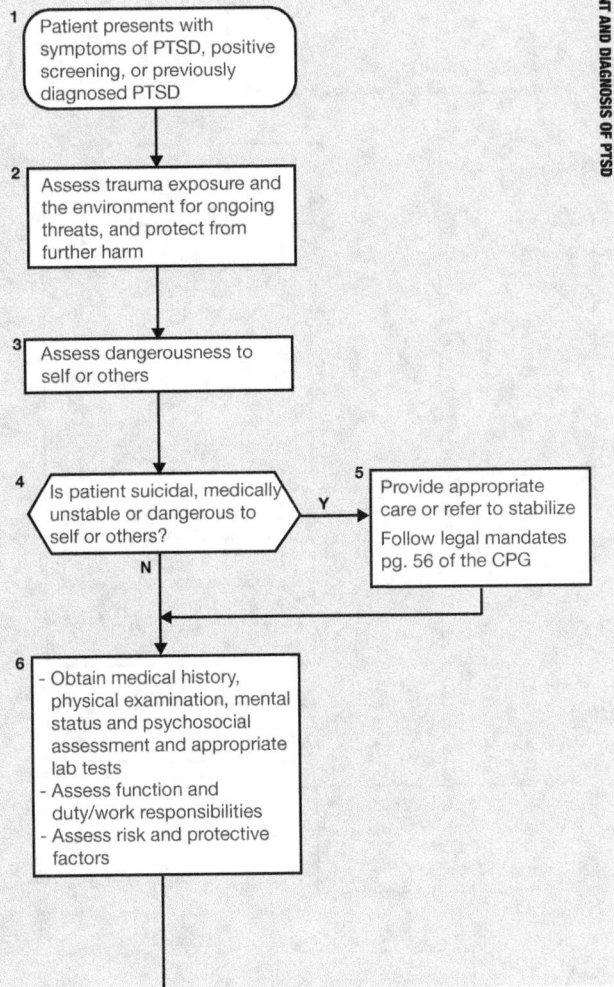

1. Patient presents with symptoms of PTSD, positive screening, or previously diagnosed PTSD

2. Assess trauma exposure and the environment for ongoing threats, and protect from further harm

3. Assess dangerousness to self or others

4. Is patient suicidal, medically unstable or dangerous to self or others?

5. Provide appropriate care or refer to stabilize

   Follow legal mandates pg. 56 of the CPG

Y

N

6. - Obtain medical history, physical examination, mental status and psychosocial assessment and appropriate lab tests
   - Assess function and duty/work responsibilities
   - Assess risk and protective factors

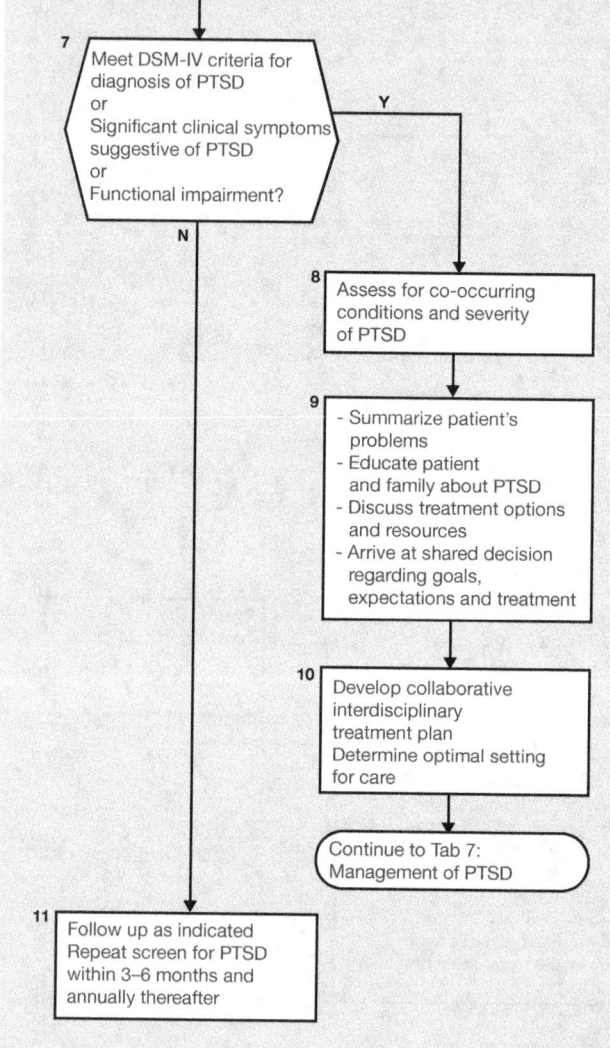

7 Meet DSM-IV criteria for diagnosis of PTSD
or
Significant clinical symptoms suggestive of PTSD
or
Functional impairment?

Y

N

8 Assess for co-occurring conditions and severity of PTSD

9
- Summarize patient's problems
- Educate patient and family about PTSD
- Discuss treatment options and resources
- Arrive at shared decision regarding goals, expectations and treatment

10 Develop collaborative interdisciplinary treatment plan
Determine optimal setting for care

Continue to Tab 7: Management of PTSD

11 Follow up as indicated
Repeat screen for PTSD within 3–6 months and annually thereafter

Page intentionally left blank

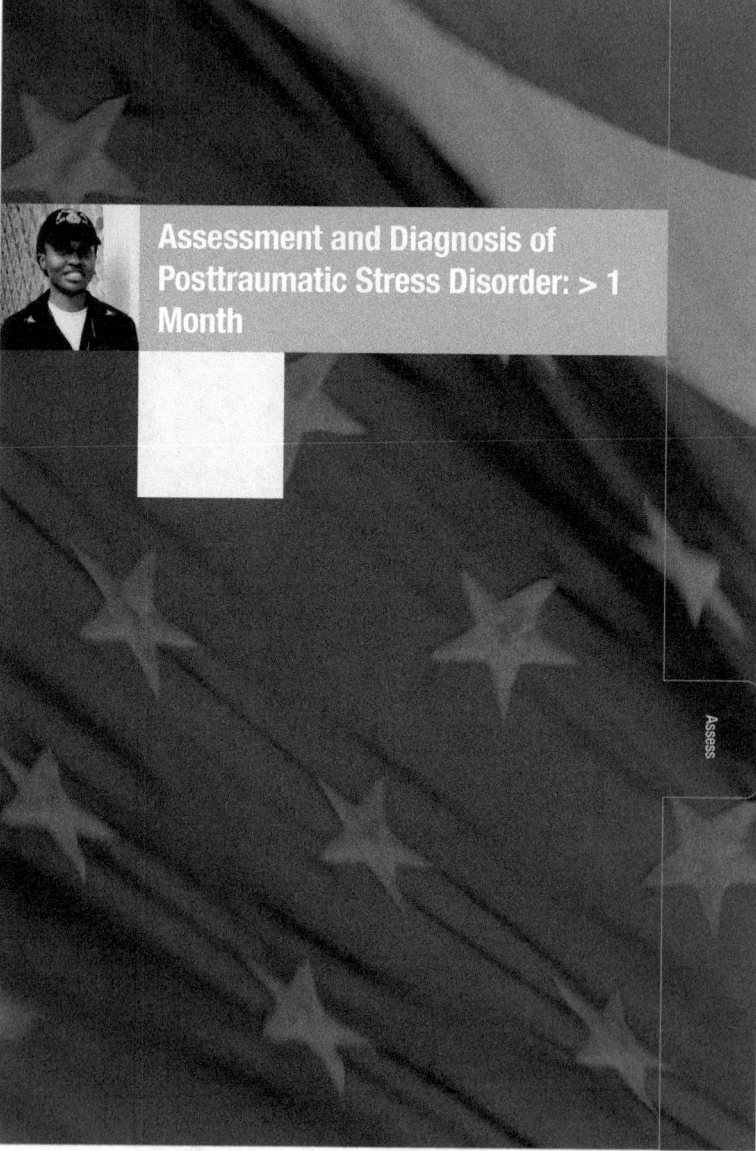

Assessment and Diagnosis of Posttraumatic Stress Disorder: > 1 Month

ASSESSMENT AND DIAGNOSIS OF POSTTRAUMATIC STRESS DISORDER: > 1 MONTH

Step A:
Initial Assessment

Step B:
Assess for Medical and Functional Status and Risk and Protective Factors

Step C:
Establish Diagnosis and Follow Up as Indicated

Step D:
Assess for Co-occurring Conditions and Severity of PTSD

Step E:
Educate Patient and Family

Step F:
Determine Optimal Setting for Management

PTSD is a clinically significant condition with symptoms continuing more than one month after exposure to a trauma that has caused significant distress or impairment in social, occupational or other important areas of functioning. Patients with PTSD may exhibit persistent re-experiencing of the traumatic event(s), persistent avoidance of stimuli associated with the trauma, numbing of general responsiveness (not present before the trauma) and persistent symptoms of increased arousal (not present before the trauma). PTSD can also have a delayed onset, which is described as a clinically significant presentation of symptoms (causing significant distress or impairment in social, occupational or other important areas of functioning) at least six months after exposure to trauma.

THREE CLUSTERS OF STRESS-RELATED SYMPTOMS
The stress-related symptoms of PTSD can be grouped by reliving or re-experiencing, avoidance and numbing, and hyperarousal symptoms.

The traumatic event is persistently re-experienced in one (or more) of the following ways:

- Recurrent and intrusive distressing recollections of the event, including images, thoughts or perceptions. Note: In young children, repetitive play may occur in which themes or aspects of the trauma are expressed
- Recurrent distressing dreams of the event. Note: In children, there may be frightening dreams without recognizable content
- Acting or feeling as if the traumatic event were recurring (includes a sense of reliving the experience, illusions, hallucinations and dissociative flashback episodes, including those that occur on awakening or when intoxicated) Note: In young children, trauma-specific reenactment may occur
- Intense psychological distress at exposure to internal or external cues that symbolize or resemble an aspect of the traumatic event
- Physiological reactivity on exposure to internal or external cues that symbolize or resemble an aspect of the traumatic event

Persistent avoidance of stimuli associated with the trauma and numbing of general responsiveness (not present before the trauma), as indicated by three (or more) of the following:

- Efforts to avoid thoughts, feelings or conversations associated with the trauma
- Efforts to avoid activities, places or people that arouse recollections of the trauma
- Inability to recall an important aspect of the trauma
- Markedly diminished interest or participation in significant activities
- Feeling of detachment or estrangement from others
- Restricted range of affect (e.g., unable to have loving feelings)
- Sense of a foreshortened future (e.g., does not expect to have a career, marriage, children or a normal life span)

Persistent symptoms of increased arousal (not present before the trauma), as indicated by two (or more) of the following:

- Difficulty falling or staying asleep
- Irritability or outbursts of anger
- Difficulty concentrating
- Hypervigilance
- Exaggerated startle response

Step A: Initial Assessment

Assess Stress-related Symptoms

- Patients who are presumed to have symptoms of PTSD or who are positive for PTSD on the initial screening should receive a thorough assessment of their symptoms that includes details such as: time of onset, frequency, course, severity, level of distress and functional impairment to guide accurate diagnosis and appropriate clinical decision-making

- Consider use of a validated self-administered checklist to ensure systematic, standardized and efficient review of the patient's symptoms and history of trauma exposure. Routine ongoing use of these checklists may allow assessment of treatment response and patient progress (see PCL-Civilian Version (PCL-C) in Tab 9: Additional Tools and Resources)

- Diagnosis of PTSD should be obtained based on a comprehensive clinical interview that assesses all the symptoms that characterize PTSD. Structured diagnostic interviews such as the Clinician Administered PTSD Scale (CAPS), may be considered

Assess Dangerousness to Self or Others

- Any assessment of PTSD should include an assessment of the patient's dangerousness to self or others. There is no set of standardized questions for this assessment
- Provide appropriate care or refer to stabilize, following legal mandates, if the patient is considered dangerous to self or others

Step B: Assess for Medical and Functional Status and Risk and Protective Factors

Medical Assessment

- Assess baseline functional and mental status, medical history to include any injury, past psychological history and current life stressors
- Take drug inventory (including over-the-counter drugs and herbals)
- Obtain physical exam and laboratory tests
- Assess for substance use or co-occurring disorders
- Complete a mental status examination
- Corroborate evaluation with family or significant other

Functional Assessment
(See table on the next page for components)

- Develop a comprehensive narrative assessment through use of standardized, targeted and validated instruments designed to assess family or relationship, work or school, and/or social functioning
- Consider the complexity and importance of the patient's job role and functional capabilities when making a return to duty or work determination
- Do not use the symptoms of PTSD alone to justify a recommendation that prevents a patient to return to work or duty

Risk and Protective Factors Assessment

- Assess for risk factors for developing PTSD
- Pay special attention to post-traumatic factors (e.g., social support, ongoing stressors, functional incapacity) that may be modified by intervention (see Tab 5 for those factors)
- **Keep in mind that PTSD symptoms may not appear until considerable time has passed – sometimes surfacing years later**

FUNCTIONAL ASSESSMENT COMPONENTS

Work	<ul><li>Is the patient unemployed or seeking employment?</li><li>If employed, have there been any changes in productivity?</li><li>Have co-workers or supervisors commented on any recent changes in appearance, quality of work or relationships?</li><li>Has the patient been tardy, less motivated, less interested?</li><li>Has the patient been more forgetful or easily distracted?</li></ul>
School	Has the patient experienced:<ul><li>Changes in grades?</li><li>Changes in relationships with friends?</li><li>Recent onset or increase in acting-out behaviors?</li><li>Recent increase in disciplinary actions?</li><li>Increased social withdrawal?</li><li>Difficulties with concentration and short-term memory?</li></ul>
Marital & Family Relationships	Has the patient experienced:<ul><li>Negative changes in relationship with significant other?</li><li>Irritability or is the patient easily angered by family members?</li><li>Withdrawal of interest in spending time with family?</li><li>Any violence within the family?</li><li>Parenting difficulties?</li><li>Sexual function difficulties?</li></ul>
Recreation	Has the patient experienced:<ul><li>Changes in recreational interests?</li><li>Decreased activity level?</li><li>Poor motivation to care for self?</li><li>Sudden decrease in physical activity?</li><li>Inability to feel pleasure?</li></ul>
Housing	Does the patient have:<ul><li>Adequate housing?</li><li>Appropriate utilities and services (electricity, plumbing and other necessities of daily life)?</li><li>A stable housing situation?</li></ul>
Legal	<ul><li>Are there outstanding warrants, restraining orders or disciplinary actions?</li><li>Is the person regularly engaging in or at risk of involvement in illegal activity?</li><li>Is the patient on probation or parole?</li><li>Is there Family Advocacy or Department of Social Services involvement?</li></ul>

Financial	Does the patient have: ■ Funds for current necessities, including food, clothing and shelter? ■ A stable source of income? ■ Significant outstanding or past-due debts, alimony or child support? ■ Access to health care and/or insurance? ■ A personally perceived need to file for bankruptcy?
Unit/ Community Involvement	■ Does the patient need to be referred to a Medical Evaluation Board, or profiled for limited duty? ■ Is the patient functional and contributing to the unit environment? ■ Is there active/satisfying involvement in a community group or organization?

Step C: Establish Diagnosis and Follow Up as Indicated

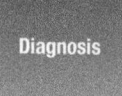

Diagnosis

■ Formulate diagnosis of stress-related disorder consistent with the current DSM criteria (see Tab 9):
  - Before initiating treatment
  - Based on a comprehensive clinical interview
■ Consider initiating treatment or referral based on a working diagnosis when diagnostic work cannot be completed
■ Refer patients with difficult or complicated presentation of the psychiatric component of PTSD to specialty care for diagnosis and treatment
■ Carefully monitor patients with partial or sub-threshold PTSD for deterioration of symptoms

Follow Up as Indicated

■ If the patient does not meet criteria for PTSD, follow up as indicated
■ Repeat screen for PTSD within three to six months and annually thereafter
■ If patient does meet criteria for PTSD, assess for co-occurring conditions and severity of PTSD (Step D)

Step D: Assess for Co-occurring Conditions and Severity of PTSD

Screen

- Recognize that medical disorders and symptoms, psychological health disorders, and psychosocial problems commonly coexist with PTSD. Screen for them during the evaluation and treatment of PTSD
- Screen for depression and other psychological disorders because of the high prevalence of co-occurring disorders in the PTSD population (For depression, the two- or nine-item Patient Health Questionnaire (PHQ-2 and PHQ-9); for SUD, the Alcohol Use Disorders Identification Test (AUDIT-C))

Assess

- Assess current and past use of substances to identify misuse or dependence (as recommended by the VA/DoD CPG for the Management of SUD)
- Assess acute and chronic pain and sleep disturbances in all patients
- Assess associated high-risk behaviors such as smoking, unsafe or risky sexual behaviors, unsafe weapon storage and dangerous driving
- Assess generalized physical and cognitive health symptoms attributed to concussion/mild traumatic brain injury (mTBI)

Manage or Refer

- Manage generalized physical and cognitive health symptoms attributed to concussion and mTBI in patients with PTSD and co-occurring diagnosis of mTBI
- Consider the existence of co-occurring conditions when deciding whether to treat patients in the primary care setting or refer them for specialty behavioral health care
- Refer patients with complicated co-occurring disorders to specialty behavioral health care or PTSD specialty care for evaluation and diagnosis

Step E: Educate Patient and Family

Help trauma survivors cope with ASD and PTSD by providing information to help them manage symptoms and benefit from treatment.

Patient and family education carries a level "C" strength of recommendation - there is no recommendation for or against the routine provision of the intervention.

Patient and family education: No recommendation for or against the routine provision of the intervention - Level "C"

- Educate about PTSD symptoms, other potential consequences of exposure to traumatic stress, practical ways of coping, co-occurring disorders with other health concerns, process of recovery and the nature of treatments

- Explain to all patients with PTSD the range of available and effective options for treatment

- Consider that patient preferences along with provider recommendations should drive the selection of treatment interventions in a shared and informed decision-making process

Topics

- Nature of PTSD symptoms: help survivor identify and label reactions

- Practical steps to cope with trauma-related problems: minimize symptom impact on functioning and quality of life

- Nature of recovery process and PTSD treatment: build motivation to participate or persist in treatment

Step F: Determine Optimal Setting for Management

The integrated treatment approach can be used to treat
PTSD and co-occurring psychological health conditions
concurrently. It is important to consider patient preferences,
severity of PTSD or co-occurring disorders, availability of
resources and service options, level of provider comfort
and experience, and the need to maintain a coordinated
continuum of care for chronic co-occurring disorders.

INTEGRATED TREATMENT APPROACH

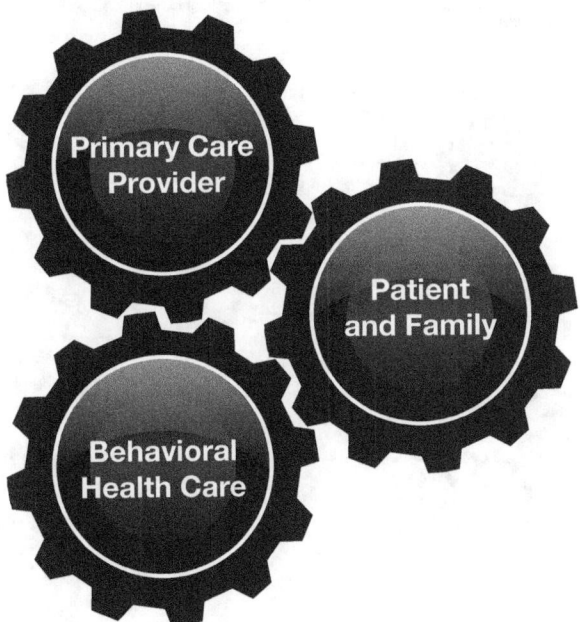

Improve Management of PTSD Symptoms When They Are Complicated by a Co-occurring SUD:

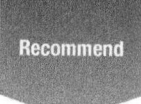

Recommend

- Recommend and offer cessation treatment to patients with nicotine dependence

Evaluate

- There is insufficient evidence to recommend for or against any specific psychosocial approach to addressing PTSD that is co-occurring with SUD
- Consider the patient's prior treatment experience and preference

Treat

- Treat concurrent SUDs consistent with VA/DoD CPGs including concurrent pharmacotherapy:
  - Addiction-focused pharmacotherapy should be discussed, considered, available and offered for all patients with alcohol dependence and/or opioid dependence
  - Once initiated, addiction-focused pharmacotherapy should be monitored for adherence and treatment response
- Promote engagement and coordination of care for both conditions by providing multiple services in the most accessible setting
- Educate patients with SUD and PTSD about the relationships between PTSD and substance abuse

Reassess

- Reassess response to treatment for SUD periodically and systematically, using standardized and valid self-report instruments and laboratory tests
- Reassess indicators of SUD treatment response to include ongoing substance use, craving, side effects of medication and emerging symptoms

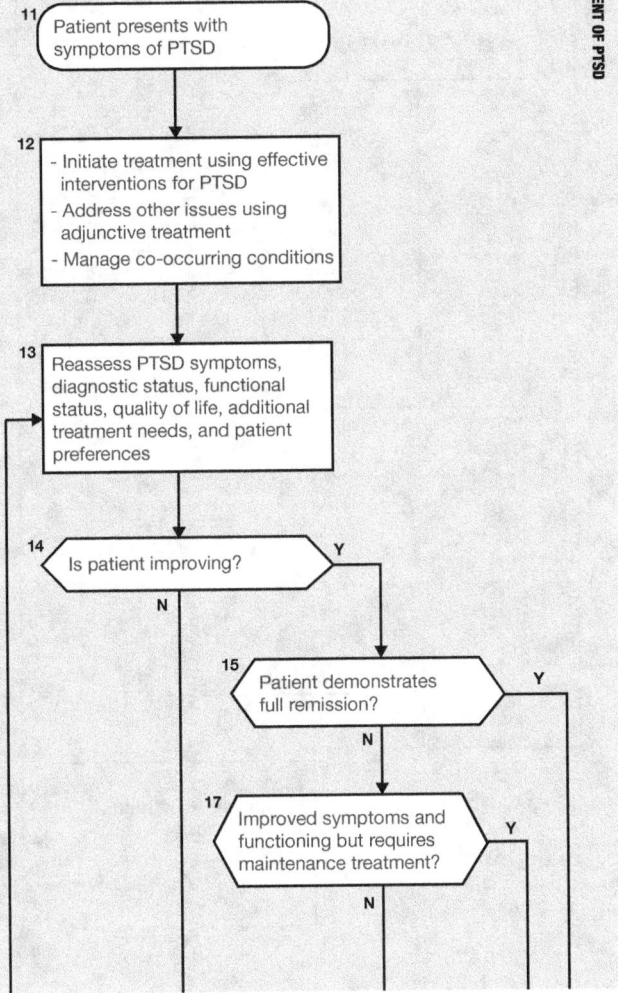

11 Patient presents with symptoms of PTSD

12
- Initiate treatment using effective interventions for PTSD
- Address other issues using adjunctive treatment
- Manage co-occurring conditions

13 Reassess PTSD symptoms, diagnostic status, functional status, quality of life, additional treatment needs, and patient preferences

14 Is patient improving?   Y

N

15 Patient demonstrates full remission?   Y

N

17 Improved symptoms and functioning but requires maintenance treatment?   Y

N

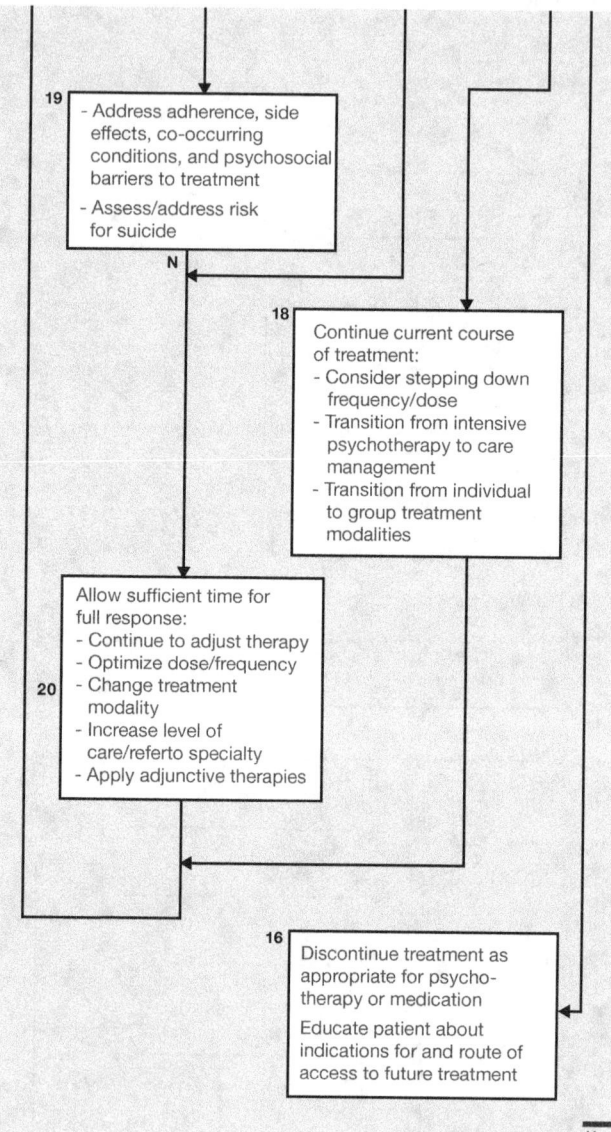

19
- Address adherence, side effects, co-occurring conditions, and psychosocial barriers to treatment
- Assess/address risk for suicide

N

18
Continue current course of treatment:
- Consider stepping down frequency/dose
- Transition from intensive psychotherapy to care management
- Transition from individual to group treatment modalities

20
Allow sufficient time for full response:
- Continue to adjust therapy
- Optimize dose/frequency
- Change treatment modality
- Increase level of care/refer to specialty
- Apply adjunctive therapies

16
Discontinue treatment as appropriate for psychotherapy or medication

Educate patient about indications for and route of access to future treatment

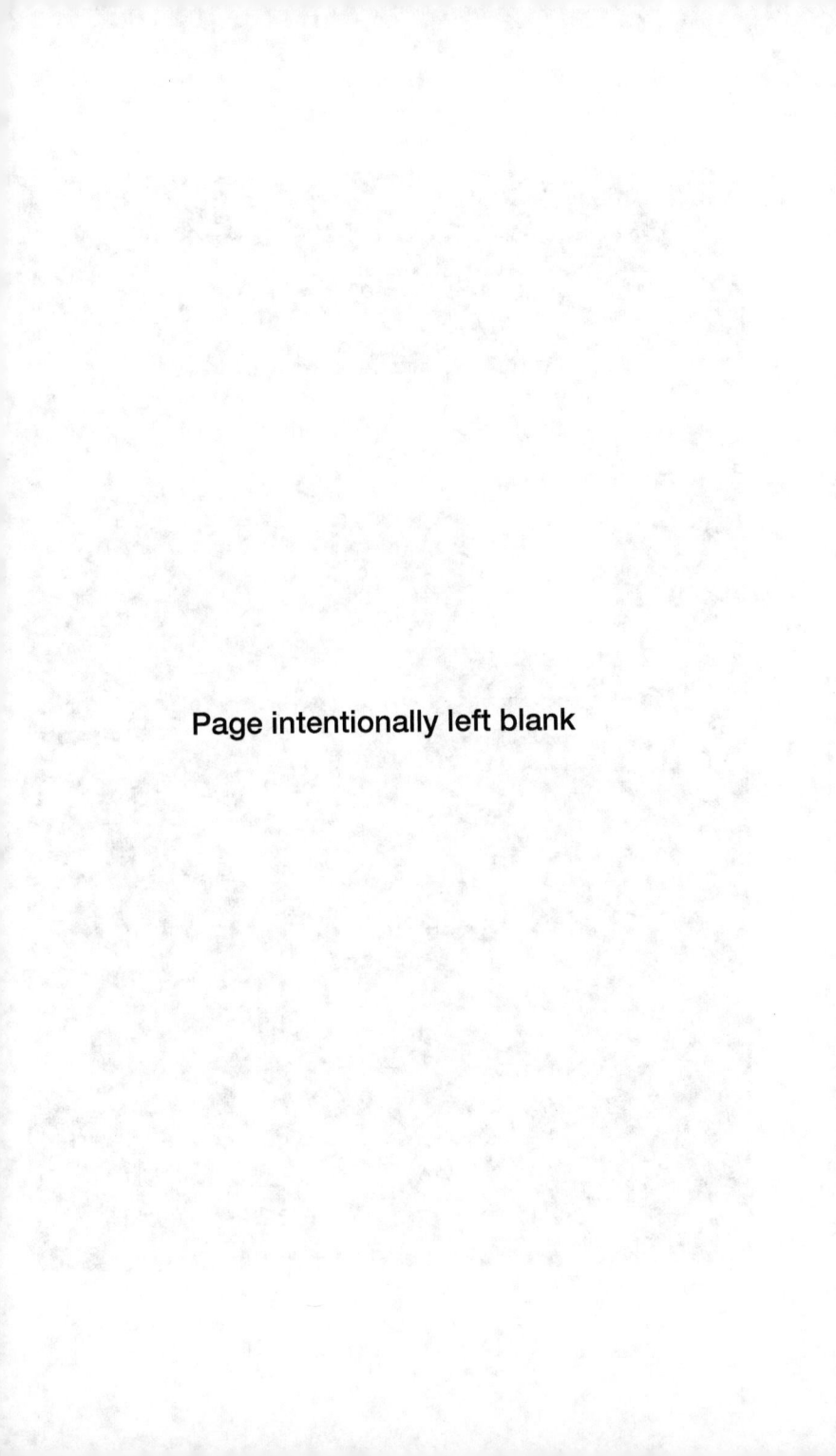
Page intentionally left blank

Management of Posttraumatic Stress Disorder: > 1 Month

MANAGEMENT OF POSTTRAUMATIC STRESS DISORDER: > 1 MONTH

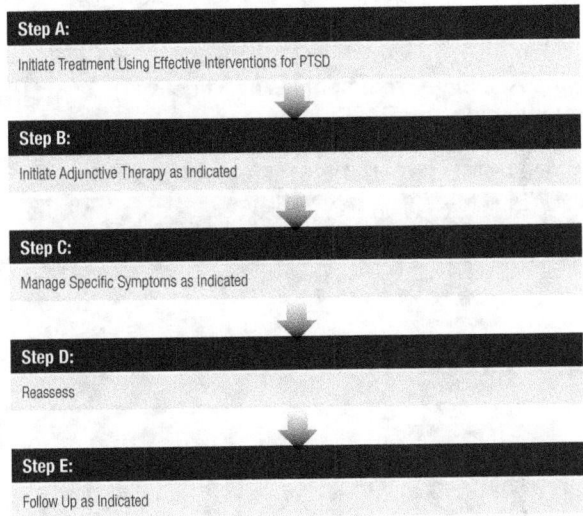

Step A:

Initiate Treatment Using Effective Interventions for PTSD

Step B:

Initiate Adjunctive Therapy as Indicated

Step C:

Manage Specific Symptoms as Indicated

Step D:

Reassess

Step E:

Follow Up as Indicated

Many treatment strategies are available to treat and relieve the burden of suffering for patient with PTSD. Therapies may be broadly divided into (1) evidence-based psychotherapies (e.g., trauma-focused therapies, stress inoculation training), (2) evidence-based pharmacotherapies (particularly selective serotonin reuptake inhibitors (SSRIs) and serotonin norepinephrine reuptake inhibitors (SNRIs)), and (3) key adjunctive or supplemental treatment modalities.

Step A: Initiate Treatment Using Effective Interventions for PTSD

PSYCHOTHERAPY INTERVENTIONS FOR TREATMENT OF PTSD

Effect = Balance of Benefit and Harm				
SR	Significant Benefit	Some Benefit	Unknown Benefit	No Benefit
A	• Trauma-focused psychotherapy that includes components of exposure and/or cognitive restructuring, or • Stress inoculation training	–	–	–
C	–	• Patient education • Imagery rehearsal therapy • Psychodynamic therapy • Hypnosis • Relaxation techniques • Group therapy	–	–

SR	Significant Benefit	Some Benefit	Unknown Benefit	No Benefit
I	–	■ Family therapy	■ Web-based CBT ■ Acceptance and commitment therapy ■ Dialectical behavioral therapy	–

SR = Strength of recommendation rating
A = Strong recommendation
C = Fair evidence but no general recommendation
I = Insufficient evidence

The core components used in the vast majority of Level A interventions have involved combinations of exposure (particularly in-vivo and imaginal/oral narrative), cognitive restructuring, relaxation/stress modulation techniques and psychoeducation. The approaches that have been most studied can be generally grouped into four main categories:

Exposure-based therapies	■ Emphasize in-vivo, imaginal, and narrative (oral and/or written) exposure, but also generally include elements of cognitive restructuring (e.g., evaluating the accuracy of beliefs about danger) as well as relaxation techniques and self-monitoring of anxiety ■ Example of therapies that include a focus on exposure include prolonged exposure therapy, brief eclectic psychotherapy, narrative therapy, written exposure therapies and many of the cognitive therapy packages that also incorporate in-vivo and imaginal/narrative exposure
Cognitive-based therapies	■ Emphasize cognitive restructuring (challenging automatic or acquired beliefs connected to the traumatic event, such as beliefs about safety or trust), but also include relaxation techniques and discussion/narration of the traumatic event either orally and/or through writing ■ Examples include cognitive processing therapy and various cognitive therapy packages tested in randomized controlled trials (RCTs)

Stress inoculation training (SIT)	• The most extensively studied specific anxiety management package in the literature • Places more emphasis on breathing retraining and muscle relaxation, but also includes cognitive elements (self-dialogue, thought stopping, role playing) and, often, exposure techniques (in-vivo exposure, narration of traumatic event)
Eye movement desensitization and reprocessing (EMDR)	• Well researched through a large number of RCTs • Closely resembles other CBT modalities in that there is an exposure component (e.g., talking about the traumatic event and/or holding distressing traumatic memories in mind without verbalizing them) combined with a cognitive component (e.g., identifying a negative cognition, an alternative positive cognition, and assessing the validity of the cognition), and relaxation/self-monitoring techniques (e.g., breathing, "body scan") • Alternating eye-movements are part of the classic EMDR technique (and the name of this type of treatment); however, comparable effect sizes have been achieved with or without eye movements or other forms of distraction or kinesthetic stimulation • Although the mechanisms of effectiveness in EMDR have yet to be determined, it is likely that they are similar to other trauma-focused exposure and cognitive-based therapies

Pharmacotherapy for PTSD

Pharmacotherapy can help patients diagnosed with PTSD. Since PTSD can be a chronic disorder, responders to pharmacotherapy may need to continue medication indefinitely; however, it is recommended that maintenance treatment be periodically reassessed. Risks and benefits of long-term pharmacotherapy should be discussed prior to starting medication and should be a continued discussion item during treatment. It is recommended to assess adherence to medication, monitor for side effects and manage adverse effects at each visit.

Head-to-head comparisons between A-level pharmacotherapies and trauma-focused psychotherapies are lacking. The use of any A-level treatment, alone or in combination, is within the standard of care. Begin initial PTSD treatment with psychotherapy and/or a first-line SSRI (e.g., paroxetine, sertraline or fluoxetine) or SNRI (e.g., venlafaxine). Reassess after two to four weeks of treatment. Although evidence does not support prazosin as monotherapy, prazosin may be initiated for patients with nightmares. If there is no response to the initial dose of antidepressant, assess adherence, consider increasing dose, increasing duration, or adding psychotherapy prior to switching to another first-line SSRI or SNRI. Reassess at four to six weeks. If initial trial of an antidepressant fails, switch to another first-line SSRI/SNRI or mirtazapine, add psychotherapy and augment with prazosin if patient has nightmares. Reassess at eight to 12 weeks. If failure after three trials, including augmentation with prazosin, then re-evaluate diagnosis and treatment, switch to a tricyclic antidepressant (TCA) and reassess as outlined above. If no response to a TCA, consider nefazodone (monitoring side effects and remaining cognizant of black box warning), or phenelzine (with careful consideration of risks). Reassess as outlined above. Consider referral to specialty care at any time during the treatment, particularly should the patient become suicidal, homicidal or clinically deteriorate to the point where they are unable to care for themselves.

Providers should give simple educational messages regarding antidepressant use (e.g., take daily, understand gradual nature of benefits, continue even when feeling better, medication may cause some transient side effects). Providers should also give specific instructions on how to address issues or concerns, and when to contact the provider, in order to increase adherence to treatment in the acute phase.

Shown in the algorithm below, pharmacotherapy is one of two primary interventions for PTSD.

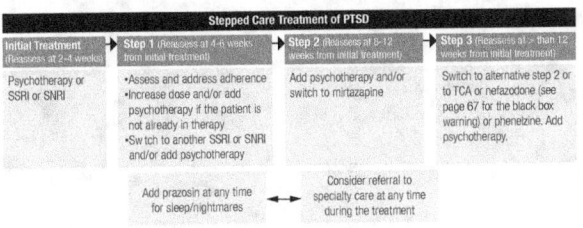

Pharmacotherapy Interventions for Treatment of PTSD: Balance of Benefit and Harm	
SR (Strength of recommendation rating)	
A (Strong recommendation)	**Significant Benefit** ■ SSRIs – paroxetine and sertraline (FDA-approved) and fluoxetine ■ SNRIs – venlafaxine
B (Fair evidence)	**Some Benefit** ■ Mirtazapine ■ Prazosin (Use for sleep/nightmares) ■ TCAs ■ Nefazodone **[Caution*]** ■ Monoamine oxidase inhibitors (phenelzine) **[Caution*]**
C (Fair evidence but no general recommendation)	**Unknown** ■ Prazosin (for global PTS symptoms)
D (Ineffective or harmful)	**No Benefit** ■ Benzodiazepines **[Harm]** ■ Tiagabine ■ Guanfacine ■ Valproate ■ Topiramate ■ Risperidone
I (Insufficient evidence)	**Unknown** ■ Atypical antipsychotics (monotherapy) - Note: Risperidone is level D ■ Atypical antipsychotics (as adjunct) ■ Conventional antipsychotics ■ Buspirone ■ Non-benzodiazepine sedative/hypnotics ■ Bupropion ■ Trazodone (as adjunct) ■ Gabapentin ■ Lamotrigine ■ Propranolol ■ Clonidine

* Attention to drug-to-drug and dietary interactions

Step B: Initiate Adjunctive Therapy as Indicated

CONSIDERATIONS

Complementary and alternative medicine (CAM)	<ul><li>**There is insufficient evidence to recommend CAM approaches as first-line treatments for PTSD**</li><li>Consider approaches that facilitate a relaxation response (e.g., mindfulness, yoga, acupuncture, massage) for adjunctive treatment of hyperarousal symptoms, although there is no evidence that these are more effective than standard stress inoculation techniques</li><li>Consider as adjunctive approaches to address some comorbid conditions (e.g., acupuncture for pain)</li><li>Consider for some patients who refuse evidence-based treatments. Providers should ensure that patients are appropriately informed and understand the evidence for effectiveness and risk-benefits of different options</li></ul>
Psychosocial rehabilitation	<ul><li>Consider psychosocial rehabilitation techniques once the client and clinician identify the following kinds of problems associated with the diagnosis of PTSD: persistent high-risk behaviors, lack of self-care or independent living skills, homelessness, interactions with a family that does not understand PTSD, social inactivity, unemployment and encounters with barriers to various forms of treatment/rehabilitation services</li><li>Determine, with patient, whether such problems are associated with core symptoms of PTSD and, if so, ensure that rehabilitation techniques are used as a contextual vehicle for alleviating PTSD symptoms</li><li>Provide concurrently or shortly after a course of treatment for PTSD, since psychosocial rehabilitation is not trauma-focused</li></ul>
Spiritual support	<ul><li>Assess for spiritual needs and facilitate access to spiritual or religious care when sought</li><li>Work with chaplains or pastoral care teams</li></ul>
Social support	<ul><li>Assess for impact of PTSD on social functioning and facilitate access to social support</li><li>Provide assistance in improving social functioning, as indicated</li></ul>

ADJUNCTIVE PROBLEM-FOCUSED METHOD AND SERVICES

If the patient and provider together conclude that the patient:		Service or training
1	Is not fully informed about aspects of health needs and does not avoid high-risk behaviors (e.g., substance use)	Provide patient education
2	Does not have sufficient self-care and independent living skills	Refer to self-care or independent living skills training services
3	Does not have safe, decent, affordable or stable housing that is consistent with treatment goals	Use and/or refer to supported housing services
4	Does not have a family that is actively supportive and/or knowledgeable about treatment for PTSD	Implement family skills training
5	Is not socially active	Implement social skills training
6	Does not have a job that provides adequate income and/or fully uses his or her training and skills	Implement vocational rehabilitation training
7	Is unable to locate and coordinate access to services, such as those listed above	Use case management services
8	Desires spiritual support	Provide access to religious or spiritual advisors and/or other resources

Step C: Manage Specific Symptoms as Indicated

This section includes recommendations regarding treatment interventions for a select list of physical symptoms that are common in patients presenting with PTSD: sleep, insomnia, pain, irritability, agitation or anger. Recommendations are based on the consensus of a working group of clinical experts.

SLEEP, PAIN AND ANGER

Sleep	<ul><li>Encourage patients to practice good sleep hygiene</li><li>Assess for insomnia</li><li>Consider adjunctive therapy for nightmares using prazosin</li><li>Reassess any significant change in sleep patterns in order to rule out worsening or new onset of co-occurring conditions</li></ul>
Insomnia	<ul><li>Monitor symptoms to assess improvement or deterioration, and reassess accordingly</li><li>Explore cause(s) for insomnia, including co-occurring conditions</li><li>Begin treatment for insomnia with non-pharmacological treatments including sleep hygiene and CBT</li><li>The selection of sleep agents for the treatment of insomnia in PTSD patients may be impacted by other treatment decisions (e.g., medications already prescribed for the treatment of PTSD, depression, TBI, pain or concurrent substance abuse/withdrawal) and social/environmental/logistical concerns:<ul><li>– Trazodone may be helpful in management of insomnia and may also supplement the action of other antidepressants</li><li>– Hypnotics are a second-line approach to the management of insomnia and should only be used for short periods of time</li><li>– Atypical antipsychotics should be avoided due to potential adverse effects but may be of value when agitation or other symptoms are severe</li><li>– Benzodiazepines should be avoided</li><li>– If nightmares remain severe, consider adjunctive treatment with prazosin</li><li>– If symptoms persist or worsen - refer for evaluation and treatment of insomnia</li></ul></li></ul>

Pain	■ Recommend pain assessment using a 0 to 10 scale ■ Obtain a thorough biopsychosocial history and assess for other medical and psychiatric problems, including risk assessment for suicidal and homicidal ideation and misuse of substances, such as drugs, alcohol, over-the-counter and prescription drugs, or narcotics ■ Assessment should include questions about the nature of the pain and likely etiology (i.e., musculoskeletal and neuropathic), locations, quality, quantity, triggers, intensity and duration of the pain, as well as aggravating and relieving factors ■ Assessment should include evaluation of the impact of pain on function and activities, pain-related disability or interference with daily activities ■ Assessment should include the identification of avoidance behaviors that contribute to emotional distress and/or impaired functioning ■ Management of pain should be multidisciplinary, addressing the physical, social, psychological and spiritual components of pain in an individualized treatment plan that is tailored to the type of pain ■ Selection of treatment options should balance the benefits of pain control with possible adverse effects (especially sedating medications) on the individual's ability to participate in, and benefit from, PTSD treatment ■ When appropriate, recommend use of non-pharmacological modalities for pain control, such as biofeedback, massage, imaging therapy, physical therapy and complimentary alternative modalities (yoga, meditation, accupuntcture)

Irritability, agitation or anger	■ Assess the nature of symptoms, severity and dangerousness. Consider using standardized anger scales, such as Spielberger's State-Trait Anger Expression Inventory, to quantify
	■ Explore for cause of symptoms and follow up to monitor change
	■ Consider referral to specialty care for counseling, or for marital or family counseling as indicated. Offer referral for
	  − Anger management therapy
	  − Training in exercise and relaxation techniques
	■ Promote participation in enjoyable activities - especially with family/loved ones
	■ Promote sleep and relaxation
	■ Avoid stimulants and other substances (e.g., caffeine, alcohol)
	■ Address pain (see pain management)
	■ Avoid benzodiazepines
	■ Consider SSRIs/SNRIs
	  − If not responding to SSRIs/SNRIs and other non-pharmacological interventions, consider low-dose anti-adrenergics or low-dose atypical antipsychotics (risperidone, quetiapine)
	  − If not responding or worsening, refer to specialty care

Additional information of management of insomnia can be found in VHA Pharmacy Benefit Management (PBM) guideline for Insomnia: pbm.va.gov/clinicalguidance/clinicalrecommendations.asp

Step D: Reassess

Symptom Assessment

- Perform a brief PTSD symptom assessment at each treatment visit
- Consider use of a validated PTSD symptom measure (e.g., PCL-C)

Treatment Assessment

- Conduct at least every 90 days
- Include a measure of PTSD symptomatology
- Consider a measure of depression symptomatology such as the PHQ-9
- Re-evaluate and measure other specific areas of treatment focus (e.g., substance abuse)
- Consider using a standard quality of life scale

Functional Assessment

- Ask patients to rate to what extent their symptoms make it difficult to engage in:
  - Vocational activities
  - Parental, spousal or other familial roles

Continued Assessment

- Patient preferences
- Treatment adherence
- Adverse treatment effects

Step E: Follow Up as Indicated

PATIENT SCENARIOS

Does not improve or status worsens (consider one)	■ Continue application of same modality at intensified dose and/or frequency ■ Change to a different treatment modality ■ Apply adjunctive therapies ■ Consider referral to adjunctive services for treatment of co-occurring disorders or behavioral abnormalities (e.g., homelessness)

Has severe symptoms or co-occurring psychiatric problems	■ Consider referrals to:
	  – Specialized PTSD programs
	  – Specialized programs for co-occurring problems and conditions
	  – Partial psychiatric hospitalization or "day treatment" programs
	  – Inpatient psychiatric hospitalization

Demonstrates partial, insufficient remission (consider one)	■ Ensure that "treatment non-response" is not due to any of the following:
	  – Non-compliance with treatment recommendations
	  – Ongoing use of alcohol or illicit substances, or suffering from ongoing insomnia or chronic pain
	  – Onset of new psychosocial stressors or overlooked co-occurring medical or psychiatric condition
	■ Continue the present treatment modality to allow sufficient time for full response
	■ Continue application of the same modality at intensified dose and/or frequency
	■ Change to a different treatment modality
	■ Apply adjunctive therapies (e.g., CAM therapies, psychosocial rehabilitation, religious support, social support)
	■ Increase level of care (e.g., refer to partial hospitalization or inpatient)
	■ Consider a referral to adjunctive services for treatment of co-occurring disorders or behavioral abnormalities

PATIENT SCENARIOS (CONTINUED)

Demonstrates improved symptoms and functioning but requires maintenance	■ Continue current course of treatment
	■ Consider stepping down the type, frequency or dose of therapy
	■ Consider:
	  – Transition from intensive psychotherapy to case management contacts
	  – Transition from individual to group treatment modalities
	  – Transition to as-needed treatment
	■ Discuss patient status and need for monitoring with primary care provider
	■ Consider a referral to adjunctive services for treatment of co-occurring disorders or behavioral abnormalities

Demonstrates remission from symptoms and there are no indications for further therapy	■ Discontinue treatment ■ Educate the patient about indications for and route of future care access ■ Monitor by primary care for relapse/exacerbation ■ Provide case management, as indicated, to address high utilization of health care resources

Medication Tables

Selective Serotonin Reuptake Inhibitors (SSRIs)

General Information for SSRIs

- **GENERAL INFORMATION:** Antidepressants, particularly SSRIs, have proven to be effective in treating PTSD and are recommended as **first-line** agents in treatment guidelines. **Paroxetine**, **sertraline** and **fluoxetine** have demonstrated an association with global symptom improvement, as well as a reduction of the specific symptoms of re-experiencing, avoidance/numbing and hyperarousal. Strongly recommend patients diagnosed with PTSD be offered monotherapy with SSRIs (**paroxetine** and **sertraline** [FDA approved] or **fluoxetine**) have the strongest support) or SNRIs (**venlafaxine** has the strongest support) for PTSD treatment.

- **SIDE EFFECTS:** Nausea, headache, diarrhea, anxiety, nervousness, sexual dysfunction, agitation, dizziness, hyponatremia or syndrome of inappropriate anti-diuretic hormone (SIADH), serotonin syndrome.

- **PREGNANCY WARNING:** All except **paroxetine** are Category C and **paroxetine** is Category D. Women planning to breast-feed should consider an antidepressant with the lowest excretion into breast milk (e.g. **paroxetine**, **sertraline**).

- **MONITORING, REFERRALS AND WARNINGS:** Monitor for hyponatremia and weight change. Monitor for sleep disturbances with **fluoxetine**.

Paroxetine (Paxil): Strongly recommend (Level A)

- **Adult oral dose:** 20-60 mg/day

Additional Information

- **Food and Drug Administration (FDA) approved for PTSD**
- Recommended as a first-line pharmacological intervention for PTSD
- May be taken with or without food
- Avoid abrupt discontinuation

Sertraline (Zoloft): Strongly recommend (Level A)

- **Adult oral dose:** 50-200 mg/day

Additional Information

- **FDA approved for PTSD**
- Recommended as a first-line pharmacological intervention for PTSD
- Avoid abrupt discontinuation

Fluoxetine (Prozac): Strongly recommend (Level A)

- **Adult oral dose:** 20-60 mg/day

Additional Information

- Recommended as a first-line pharmacological intervention for PTSD
- Need for downward dosage titration lessened by long half-life
- Long half-life can prolong side effects after discontinuing therapy but can also limit the effect of a missed dose

Selective Norepinephrine Reuptake Inhibitors (SNRIs)

General Information for SNRIs

- **GENERAL INFORMATION:** Strongly recommend patients diagnosed with PTSD be offered monotherapy with SSRIs as described in previous section or SNRIs (**venlafaxine**) has the strongest support) for PTSD treatment. **Venlafaxine** has demonstrated an association with global symptom improvement as well as reduction of the specific symptoms of re-experiencing, avoidance/numbing and hyperarousal. **Duloxetine** and **desvenlafaxine** have not been studied for use in PTSD.

- **PREGNANCY WARNING: Venlafaxine** is Category C.

- **MONITORING, REFERRALS AND WARNINGS:** Monitor cholesterol, sodium (Na) levels, blood pressure (BP), heart rate (HR) and those with elevated intraocular pressure.

Venlafaxine (Effexor): Strongly recommend (Level A)	Additional Information
Adult oral dose: 150–375 mg/day	<ul><li>Recommended as a first-line pharmacological intervention for PTSD</li><li>Extended release (XR) formula used in studies establishing efficacy</li><li>Take with food</li><li>Need to taper **venlafaxine** to prevent rebound signs or symptoms</li><li>**Side effects:** Headache, insomnia, somnolence, nervousness, dizziness, anorexia, worsening hypertension in patients with pre-existing hypertension</li></ul>

Tricyclic Antidepressants (TCAs)

General Information for TCAs

- **GENERAL INFORMATION:** Clinical trials support the efficacy of TCAs for neuropathic pain in patients with PTSD. TCAs are second-line treatment options for PTSD. Administer at bedtime to reduce daytime sedation. Therapy should not be abruptly discontinued in patients receiving high doses for prolonged periods of time. Protriptyline (Vivactil) and clomipramine (Anafranil) have not been studied in PTSD. Amitriptyline and imipramine have demonstrated an association with global symptom improvement, re-experiencing and hyperarousal. May be useful in insomnia.

- **CONTRAINDICATIONS:** Acute myocardial infarction (MI) within three months

- **RELATIVE CONTRAINDICATIONS:** Coronary artery disease, prostatic enlargement

- **SIDE EFFECTS:** Dry mouth, dry eyes, constipation, orthostatic hypotension, tachycardia, ventricular arrhythmias, weight gain and drowsiness. Photosensitivity may occur.

- **PREGNANCY WARNING:** All medications listed above are Category C. Women planning to breast-feed should consider an antidepressant with the lowest excretion into breast milk (nortriptyline).

- **MONITORING, REFERRALS AND WARNINGS: Elevated blood levels can cause potentially lethal cardiac conduction delays. Polypharmacy with TCAs requires checking of drug–drug interactions.** Monitor weight, BP and HR before and during initial therapy. Orthostatic hypotension and related dizziness is a common occurrence, recommend getting up slowly to avoid dizziness. Monitor electrocardiogram (ECG) in older adults and those with cardiac disease. Monitor for signs of infection and obtain a complete blood count (CBC) if fever or sore throat occurs. May alter glucose control, use caution in diabetics. TCAs should be used cautiously. If the use of TCAs is necessary, nortriptyline and desipramine should be considered first. Avoid using amitriptyline and imipramine in the elderly. Avoid use in patients with glaucoma, urinary retention, cardiovascular disease, cognitive impairment and at risk for suicide.

Amitriptyline (Formerly known as Elavil or Endep): Recommend (Level B)

- **Adult oral dose:** 150-300 mg/day

Additional Information

- Considered as monotherapy second-line treatment option for PTSD
- Demonstrated positive outcomes
- Therapeutic blood concentrations are not established for PTSD
- Blood levels can be monitored for toxicity
- Higher rate of sedation, anticholinergic and hypotensive effects than **desipramine** and **nortriptyline**
- Higher doses may be required for smokers taking amitriptyline due to increased metabolism

Imipramine (Tofranil): Recommend (Level B)

- **Adult oral dose:** 150-300 mg/day

Additional Information

- Considered as monotherapy second-line treatment option for PTSD
- Demonstrated positive outcomes
- Therapeutic blood concentrations are not established for PTSD
- Blood levels can be monitored for toxicity
- Therapeutic levels for depression (in conjunction with psychiatry consultation) 200-350 ng/ml
- Higher rate of sedation, anticholinergic and hypotensive effects than **desipramine** and **nortriptyline**

Desipramine (Norpramin): Recommend (Level B)

- **Adult oral dose:** 100-300 mg/day

Additional Information

- Equal efficacy and fewer side effects than **amitriptyline** and **imipramine**
- Lower rate of sedation, anticholinergic and hypotensive effects than **amitriptyline** and **imipramine**
- Therapeutic blood concentrations are not established for PTSD
- Blood levels can be monitored for toxicity
- Therapeutic levels for depression (in conjunction with psychiatry consultation) 125-300 ng/ml

Nortriptyline (Pamelor), (Formerly known as Aventyl): Recommend (Level B)

- **Adult oral dose:** 50-150 mg/day

Additional Information

- Equal efficacy and fewer side effects than **amitriptyline** and **imipramine**
- Lower rate of sedation, anticholinergic and hypotensive effects than **amitriptyline** and **imipramine**
- Therapeutic blood concentrations are not established for PTSD
- Blood levels can be monitored for toxicity
- Therapeutic levels for depression (in conjunction with psychiatry consultation) 50-175 ng/ml

Sympatholytics

General Information for Sympatholytics

- **GENERAL INFORMATION:** Insufficient evidence to support **prazosin** use as monotherapy in PTSD management
- **PREGNANCY WARNING:** Pregnancy Category C. Breast-feeding effects are unknown with **prazosin**.
- **MONITORING, REFERRALS AND WARNINGS:** Monitor HR and BP. Use caution with **prazosin** for orthostatic hypotension.

Prazosin (Minipres): Fair evidence but no general recommendation for global PTSD symptoms (Level C)	Additional Information
- **Adult oral dose:** Initial 2 mg QHS and then titrate as tolerated up to 10-15mg QHS	- **Contraindications:** Hypersensitivity to **quinazolines (doxazosin, tamsulosin, terazosin)** - Primarily used for management of recurrent distressing dreams/nightmares (level B) - First dose syncope

Other Pharmacological Interventions for Treatment of PTSD

BENZODIAZEPINES: There is evidence against the use of benzodiazepines in PTSD management, as harm may outweigh benefit (Level D strength of recommendation). Strongly recommend against the use of benzodiazepines for prevention of ASD or the treatment of PTSD.

ATYPICAL ANTIPSYCHOTICS: VA/DoD PTS CPG states that the evidence does not support the use of atypical antipsychotics as a monotherapy for PTSD. The VA/DoD PTS CPG recommends against the use of risperidone as an adjunctive medication for PTSD; there is insufficient evidence to recommend for or against other atypical antipsychotics as an adjunctive treatment for PTSD.

TYPICAL ANTIPSYCHOTICS: There is insufficient evidence to recommend the use of typical antipsychotics as monotherapy or adjunct for PTSD.

ANTICONVULSANTS: The evidence does not support the use of anticonvulsants as a monotherapy for PTSD.

BUPROPION, TRAZODONE: There is insufficient evidence to recommend the use of these medications as monotherapy in PTSD. Trazodone may be useful as adjunctive therapy in PTSD.

ANTIDEPRESSANT BLACK BOX WARNING: Antidepressants may increase the risk of suicidal thinking and behavior (suicidality) as compared to treatment with placebos in young adults 18 to 24 years old, particularly in the first one to two months of treatment. Patients of all ages who are started on antidepressant therapy for both psychiatric and non-psychiatric conditions should be monitored appropriately and observed closely for clinical worsening, suicidality, or unusual changes in behavior. Short-term studies did not show an increase in the risk of suicidality with antidepressants compared to placebo in adults beyond age 24. There was a reduction in risk with antidepressants compared to placebo in adults age 65 and older.

Refer to the pharmaceutical manufacturer's literature for full prescribing information. The tables list commonly prescribed medications for PTSD. The decision to use one medication over another should be based on individual patient factors, symptom complaints and potential side effects as well as evidence from research. Please see the CPG for the complete drug interaction listing.

Page intentionally left blank

Additional Tools
& Resources

Tab 9:
ADDITIONAL TOOLS & RESOURCES

This tab includes information on:
- DSM-IV-TR Criteria for ASD
- DSM-IV-TR Criteria for PTSD
- Specifiers
- The PCL-C
- Additional Resources for Providers and Patients

PTS CRITERIA AND SPECIFIERS

DSM-IV-TR Criteria:

DSM-IV-TR Criteria for ASD

A The person has been exposed to a traumatic event in which both of the following were present:
- The person experienced, witnessed or was confronted with an event or events that involved actual or threatened death or serious injury.
- The person's response involved intense fear, helplessness or horror.

B Either while experiencing or after experiencing the distressing event, the person has at least three of the following symptoms:
- A subjective sense of numbing, detachment or absence of emotional responsiveness
- A reduction in awareness of his or her surroundings
- Derealization
- Depersonalization
- Dissociative amnesia (i.e., inability to recall an important aspect of the trauma)

C The traumatic event is re-experienced in at least one of the following ways:
- Recurrent images
- Thoughts
- Dreams
- Illusions
- Flashback episodes or a sense of reliving the experience
- Distress on exposure to reminders of the traumatic event

D The patient avoids the stimuli that arouse recollections of the trauma.

E The patient has marked symptoms of anxiety or increased arousal.

F The disturbance causes clinically significant distress or impairment in social or occupational areas of functioning, or it impairs the person's ability to pursue some necessary task.

G The disturbance lasts for a minimum of two days and a maximum of four weeks and occurs within four weeks of the traumatic event.

H The disturbance is not better accounted for by brief psychotic disorder and is not merely an exacerbation of a preexisting Axis I or Axis II disorder, substance or general medical condition.

DSM-IV-TR Criteria for PTSD

A The person has been exposed to a traumatic event in which both of the following were present:

- The person experienced, witnessed or was confronted with an event that involved actual or threatened death or serious injury or a threat to the physical integrity of others
- The person's response involved intense fear, helplessness or horror

B The traumatic event is persistently re-experienced in at least one of the following ways:

- Recurrent and intrusive distressing recollections of the event, including images, thoughts or perceptions
- Recurrent distressing dreams of the event
- Acting or feeling as if the traumatic event were recurring, including a sense of reliving the experience, illusions, hallucinations and flashback episodes
- Intense psychological distress at exposure to cues that symbolize an aspect of the traumatic event
- Physiologic reactivity on exposure to cues that symbolize or resemble an aspect of the traumatic event

C The person persistently avoids stimuli associated with the trauma and has numbing of general responsiveness including at least three of the following:

- Efforts to avoid thoughts, feelings or conversations associated with the trauma
- Efforts to avoid activities, places or people that arouse recollections of the trauma
- Inability to recall an important aspect of the trauma
- Markedly diminished interest or participation in significant activities
- Feeling of detachment or estrangement from others
- Restricted range of affect
- A sense of a foreshortened future

D Persistent symptoms of increased arousal are indicated by at least two of the following:

- Difficulty falling or staying asleep
- Irritability or outbursts of anger
- Difficulty concentrating
- Hypervigilance
- Exaggerated startle response

E Duration of the disturbance is more than one month

F The disturbance causes clinically significant distress or impairment in social, occupational or other important areas of functioning

SPECIFIERS:

Course	**ASD**	■ Two days to one month
	PTSD: Acute	■ Fewer than three months
	PTSD: Chronic	■ Greater than three months
	PTSD: With Delayed Onset	■ More than six months have passed between the event and symptom onset

Source: American Psychiatric Association: Diagnostic and Statistical Manual of Mental Disorders, 4th ed, text rev. Washington, DC, American Psychiatric Association, 2000.

PTSD CheckList – Civilian Version (PCL-C)

Client's Name:_____

Instruction to patient: Below is a list of problems and complaints that veterans sometimes have in response to stressful life experiences. Please read each one carefully, put an "X" in the box to indicate how much you have been bothered by that problem in *the last month*.

1 = Not at all	2 = A little bit	3 = Moderately	4 = Quite a bit	5 = Extremely

RESPONSE

	1	2	3	4	5
1. Repeated, disturbing memories, thoughts or images of a stressful experience from the past?	1	2	3	4	5
2. Repeated, disturbing dreams of a stressful experience from the past?	1	2	3	4	5
3. Suddenly acting or feeling as if a stressful experience were happening again (as if you were reliving it)?	1	2	3	4	5
4. Feeling very upset when something reminded you of a stressful experience from the past?	1	2	3	4	5
5. Having physical reactions (e.g., heart pounding, trouble breathing or sweating) when something reminded you of a stressful experience from the past?	1	2	3	4	5
6. Avoid thinking about or talking about a stressful experience from the past or avoid having feelings related to it?	1	2	3	4	5
7. Avoid activities or situations because they remind you of a stressful experience from the past?	1	2	3	4	5
8. Trouble remembering important parts of a stressful experience from the past?	1	2	3	4	5
9. Loss of interest in things that you used to enjoy?	1	2	3	4	5
10. Feeling distant or cut off from other people?	1	2	3	4	5
11. Feeling emotionally numb or being unable to have loving feelings for those close to you?	1	2	3	4	5
12. Feeling as if your future will somehow be cut short?	1	2	3	4	5
13. Trouble falling or staying asleep?	1	2	3	4	5
14. Feeling irritable or having angry outbursts?	1	2	3	4	5
15. Having difficulty concentrating?	1	2	3	4	5
16. Being "super alert" or watchful on guard?	1	2	3	4	5
17. Feeling jumpy or easily startled?	1	2	3	4	5

PCL-M for DSM-IV (11/1/94) Weathers, Litz, Huska, & Keane National Center for PTSD - Behavioral Science Division

PTSD CheckList – Civilian Version (PCL-C)

The PCL is a standardized self-report rating scale for PTSD comprising 17 items that correspond to the key symptoms of PTSD. Two versions of the PCL exist: 1) PCL-M is specific to PTSD related to military experiences and 2) PCL-C is applied generally to any traumatic event.

The PCL can be easily modified to fit specific time frames or events. For example, instead of asking about "the past month," questions may ask about "the past week" or be modified to focus on events specific to a deployment.

How is the PCL completed?

- The PCL is self-administered
- Respondents indicate how much they have been bothered by a symptom over the past month using a five-point (1–5) scale, circling their responses. Responses range from 1 Not at All – 5 Extremely

How is the PCL Scored?

1. Add up all items for a total severity score or

2. Treat response categories 3–5 (Moderately or above) as symptomatic and responses 1–2 (below Moderately) as non-symptomatic, then use the following DSM criteria for a diagnosis:
   - Symptomatic response to at least 1 "B" item (Questions 1–5),
   - Symptomatic response to at least 3 "C" items (Questions 6–12), and
   - Symptomatic response to at least 2 "D" items (Questions 13–17)

Are results valid and reliable?

- Two studies of both Vietnam and Persian Gulf theater veterans show that the PCL is both valid and reliable (Additional references are available from the Deployment Health Clinical Center (DHCC))

What additional follow-up is available?

- All military health system beneficiaries with health concerns they believe are deployment-related are encouraged to seek medical care
- Patients should be asked, "Is your health concern today related to a deployment?" during all primary care visits
- If the patient replies "yes," the provider should follow the Post-Deployment Health Clinical Practice Guideline (PDH-CPG) and supporting guidelines available through the DHCC and pdhealth.mil

Clinical practice guidelines and clinical support tools can be accessed at healthquality.va.gov and https://www.qmo.amedd.army.mil:

- The full VA/DoD PTS guideline, as well as updated VA/DoD CPGs for additional psychological health disorders including bipolar disorder, major depressive disorder, PTSD and SUD
- Provider, patient and family clinical support tools are available for:
    - PTSD
    - Major depression
    - Bipolar disorder
    - mTBI
    - Opioid therapy
    - SUD
    - Various chronic medical diseases/conditions

Resources for service members, veterans and providers include:

- **National Center for PTSD (NCPTSD)**
  ptsd.va.gov
- **Center for the Study of Traumatic Stress (CSTS)**
  centerforthestudyoftraumaticstress.org
- **RESPECT-Mil**
  pdhealth.mil
- **After Deployment**
  afterdeployment.org
- **My HealtheVet**
  myhealth.va.gov
- **Military OneSource**
  militaryonesource.com
- **VA Military Sexual Trauma Counseling**
  vetcenter.va.gov
- **Our Military**
  ourmilitary.mil
- **Real Warriors**
  realwarriors.net
- **VA's Make the Connection**
  maketheconnection.net